God’s Garden,

My Life

God’s Garden, My Life

by: Bonnie J. Lee

Tome Publishing
Maryville, Tennessee

For additional copies of this book, please contact:

Bonnie J. Lee

Email: tblee1@bellsouth.net

Copyright (c) 2005 by Bonnie J. Lee
All rights reserved. This material is not to be reproduced, stored or transmitted in any manner or form without prior permission from this author.

ISBN 1-928672-04-3

Published by:

Tome Publishing
909 Brown School Road
Maryville TN 37804

Cover design by Deborah Taylor

TABLE OF CONTENTS

God's Garden

INTRODUCTION

In my gardens I have dealt with soil which was not rich enough to grow healthy plants, and weeds which sometimes were invasive enough to keep the plants I wanted in the bed from growing as they should.

I have found that adding proper fertilizer, compost, and mulch into that soil makes a tremendous difference. The climate zones where I have lived have determined what plants would grow best. Experience has taught me that adequate watering makes beautiful lawns and causes plants to perform as they have been programmed. When planting a vegetable garden, critters have beat me to the produce. On and on were my lessons.

Over the years, I saw so many scriptures in the Bible which I directly applied to my experiences in gardening. I began to make note of them, and the Holy Spirit continually gave me new insight into how to apply this fertilizer/nourishment to the garden of my own heart.

From all of this a Bible study was developed, including quotes from many authors.

It is my hope that the reader's own life's garden will be enriched by these experiences and applications, producing beauty and fruit to share in the climate zone where you find yourself planted.

Bonnie J. Lee

<u>The Garden in Our Hearts</u>

Within each of us lies a garden,
You need only look inside,
It lies within our hearts
Where love and hope abide.
It's there in all its splendor
Though some eyes cannot see
The beauty there within themselves,
So they choose not to believe.

But the garden's there, I've seen it
Every time I've witnessed love,
Every time a heart has reached out
With compassion from above.
Each and every act of kindness
Acts of giving, sharing, too,
All represent a flower
There inside of me and you.

But each garden must be tended
It needs love and special care,
An abundance of pure water
That is only found in prayer.
For the Master Gardener knows
Of every heart of every bloom
And it's His hope and desire
In your garden you've made room,
So that He may tend the flowers
And may pull a weed or two,
For without the Master Gardener
Hearts have flowers, far too few.

Gina Laurin, *New Hope Books*

IN APPRECIATION

My heartfelt thanks must be given specifically to Deborah Taylor for her encouragement to publish this compilation of insights and lessons given to me over many years. To Kim and Steve McKee and to Linda Denyer, appreciation for their expertise in editing and correcting the text. To Pastor Steve Streeter and his wife, Shirley, who sat through a class I taught at our church and gave me the sense that the lessons would be helpful to many.

Lastly, hugs and kisses to my husband, Ted, who has supported my efforts, urging me to go ahead with what I felt the Lord was leading me to do.

I ask the Lord to bless you all abundantly.

Bonnie

CHAPTER ONE

DIGGING IN THE DIRT

Source: *The Tennessee Master Gardener Handbook*, University of Tennessee Agricultural Extension Service.

You can drop some seeds in the dirt, cover them a little bit, water them, and hope they'll produce a beautiful flower that will give great enjoyment. You can buy an expensive bush, dig a hole and plant it, water it, and hope it will grow into a gorgeous bush. But if that "dirt" is lacking in structure, at best you'll get a sickly little flower and a shrub that won't give you the results you want.

Soil is defined as finely divided rock mixed with vegetable or animal matter, constituting that portion of the surface of the earth in which plants grow.

Good soil is the most important element in your garden. Soil is a medium to support plant growth and development. It determines the health of your plants. Soil can limit growth. It is made up of sand, silt, or clay.

Soil fertility is the quality of a soil that enables it to supply a plant with the nutrients it needs to grow. Soil in the East Tennessee region consists of steep, stony land that is shallow, acidic, and low in fertility. Because much of the soil in this region is low in organic matter (oxidized iron is what makes it red), it is often necessary to add organic material which serves important functions in maintaining plant life, storage of water and nutrients, and reducing soil erosion. As the organic matter decomposes in the soil, it opens the soil up to allow nutrients to penetrate, as well as water to get to roots.

Example: In our heavy clay soil, which is rich in nutrients, unless there is sufficient organic material, the roots will rot (actually suffocate) because water cannot pass through. In sandy soil, if there is not enough organic material, water will pass through so quickly the plant will not get a sufficient amount. Organic matter gives the soil structure and makes it easy to work. It will have good "tilth" or workability.

A soil test will let you know what kind of soil you have and what nutrients it needs. This is done by digging up some soil in about six areas of your garden (or lawn, if that is what you're testing). Dig down about 6" with a small shovel or spade and put a dry sample from each area in a container, removing any organic debris, rocks, and trash. Mix up the samples and fill the sample box. Indicate on the accompanying sheet where the soil came from (ex. "front yard"). Follow the directions for mailing, add your check, and send it to the laboratory indicated on the kit from where your sample box and sheet came. (Your local Agricultural Extension office has the forms you need along with instructions about where to send them.) In a few weeks you will get an analysis of that soil sample showing what is lacking (if anything) and giving instruction about what to add.

The kinds of weeds present in your soil can be an indicatorof the type of soil you have. Example: red sorrel (sheep sorrel) indicates dry, sandy, sterile, or gravelly soil that is acidic and low in nitrogen. Improving the soil pH to between 6 and 7, by adding lime and organic matter, will help stop the growth of these invasive weeds which multiply by underground root runners.

Sandy loam and medium loam are the best garden soils because they have a nice balance between sand and clay. Their value is from the decayed vegetable matter they often contain. Since plants store nutrients in their tissues, dead plant matter contains some nutrients which may eventually become available to growing plants.

A garden soil without a few shortcomings is rare. Here in the East, the soil deficiencies in one garden are usually different from those in the gardens in the next block. Some deficiencies are minor and easy to correct; others are deep-seated. Each type of soil must be treated individually. After a few seasons of working in your soil you will learn its characteristics.

Deficient soil can be changed by using manures, which are readily available in this area. Manure contains many essential elements.

Compost is another great way of amending your soil. It is usually richer because it is made up of a variety of materials, such as kitchen scraps (no animal material), leaves, weeds you've pulled, as well as grass clippings and small branches (which take a little longer to break down). Compost made from whole plant parts is usually richer in nutrients than that made only from leaves or other plant extremities. These nutrients, released by composting, come from all parts of a plant, especially roots and stems. Compost is an excellent supplier of organic matter. (Note: the smaller the particles of material you add, the sooner they will break down.) (See chapter 6: "Mulching and Composting.")

It is important for you to learn the general characteristics of your soil: sandy, loamy, or clay. Is it high or low in organic material?

Hard soil is heavy clay: sticky when wet, brick-like, and cracked when dry. It is, however, richest in nutrients. Adding material like manure and compost makes the soil crumble more easily so roots can penetrate the soil and absorb those nutrients.

Your soil may be too shallow. There may be very little top soil. It may be rocky. There may be a hardpan; the roots cannot grow deep. Water won't drain as fast as necessary. To get maximum benefit, either bore through the hardpan to more soft and spreadable soil, or add lots of topsoil, or build raised beds.

Garden plants get most of their nutrients from the top foot of soil. For this reason, plants are sensitive to the condition of the soil surface. (This is also where you will find earthworms, which do not like to have the soil disturbed.) If the soil becomes compacted, the roots near the surface receive less oxygen and water, and may die. Trees and shrubs growing in compacted soil develop surface roots. These can easily be damaged when tilling or preparing the soil for plants.

Incidentally, did you know that earthworms have tiny hairs that help them crawl? And that some of them have as many as 150 segments to their bodies? Contrary to an old wives' tale, they cannot grow a new body if cut in two; they die! Worms aerate the soil with their tunnels. They also carry organic matter to the subsoil and to the surface to be enriched. Red worms are the best worms to add to your compost pile and are available at bait stores for little money. The more earthworms you find in your soil, the better. They somehow "know" where the good soil is! Earthworms just "appear" when the soil is loose enough for them to get through, and they add richness by digesting available organic matter. So when you find earthworms, be blessed! They're helping your soil.

Lee Reich of *The Associated Press* wrote a November article "Prepare soil now for spring planting." It stated:

> "Preparing the ground now for planting lets you get your first seeds into that ground earlier in spring. Although wet soil often delays spring soil preparation, in fall the soil

is usually just right for digging–moist, but not sodden. Fall tillage is less work because your goal is to leave the soil in rough clods, rather than to create a fine seedbed. Freezing and thawing in winter breaks up those clods so that simple raking crumbles them into a smooth seedbed.

"An even easier way to avoid delay in spring planting is by not tilling at all. We till soils for aeration, but that's only needed because we compact soils by walking on them. If you will lay out your garden in permanent beds and paths, you never have to walk where you plant, therefore the soil will never need tilling.

"Whether or not you till your soil, now is also a good time to get a jump on weeds. Waiting until spring to till gives annual weeds plenty of time to ripen and disperse their seeds, and perennial weeds time to get a strong foothold. Either hoe weeds to death or pull them out, roots and all. Garden edges need special attention to prevent creeping weeds, such as quackgrass and ground ivy, from sneaking in.

"Fall is also a good season to make and use compost. All at once, so much compostable material is available: tomato vines, rotted fruits and vegetables, trimmings and pits from canning and freezing, tree leaves and grass clippings. A compost pile built this fall should be thoroughly broken down and ready for use within a year (unless you turn it more often). Use compost to blanket untilled beds. If you till, spread compost over the surface after you till. (See the chapter on compost.) "An inch or two of compost each year supplies much of the nutrition that plants need, but your garden might also need more concentrated fertilizers and, perhaps, lime.

"Fall is also a good time to apply lime and fertilizer; especially organic fertilizers, which are less likely than synthetic fertilizers to leach out of the soil by spring. Soybean meal is an organic fertilizer that is rich in nitrogen (7 percent) and inexpensive. Usually, one feeding, at the rate of 6 cups per hundred square feet, is all that's needed."

SPIRITUAL APPLICATION

God is the bed into which my life's garden is planted.

My life is a garden,
Your life is a garden.
Is it waste, untilled, and wild?
Like an untaught, untrained child?
Or is it good soil under the Master's hand?
Is my soul His own cherished land?
Is it grown thick with thistles and weed?
Or has it been sown with His good seed?
What is the harvest that comes from this life?
Goodness and love, or hatred and strife?
O Lord, take this stony ground of mine.
Make it all, completely Thine.
Only then can it ever yield
The pleasant fruits of a godly field.
Anonymous

God's greatest desire for us is that we are His garden. In the book of Song of Solomon, He states that in His garden He finds perfumes and spices, the finest fruits, water for the thirsty, and bubbling brooks. (Song of Solomon 4:12-16)

The first vocation was gardening. God gave His first creations a garden to live in and tend. He wants to restore for us, in our hearts, a garden where He is welcome; where beauty grows. He wants us to maintain our garden.

The soil of my heart's garden determines the health of the "plants" and "fruits" in my life. Earlier, our text stated that soil can limit growth.

Matthew 12:33-35 GNB states: "To have good fruit

you must have a healthy tree. If you have a poor tree, you will have bad fruit. A tree is known by the fruit it bears. For the mouth speaks what the heart is full of. A good person brings good things out of his treasure of good things; a bad person brings bad things out of his treasure of bad things." Poor soil will not grow a healthy tree.

Luke 6:43 states: "A healthy tree does not bear bad fruit, nor does a poor tree bear good fruit. Every tree is known by the fruit it bears; you do not pick figs from thorn bushes or gather grapes from bramble bushes. A good person brings good out of the treasure of good things in his heart; a bad person brings bad out of his treasure of bad things. For the mouth speaks what the heart is full of."

Peggy Benson has written, "Before anything can be planted, the soil must be ready. We must allow the softening mulch of God's forgiveness to give air and breath to the soil of our hearts. Prejudices, taught in our childhood or imposed by our society, must be released. Fear must be replaced by trust, and suspicion by childlike hope and acceptance. These changes in the soil will not come easily or without sweat, but any good gardener knows that preparing the soil is the most important of all labors. It gives the seeds a chance to grow and eventually, to exhibit all that is hidden in their complex genetic structure."

The heart is the center of the human will, and we read about the hardened heart (Exodus 4:21), one that is yielded (Joshua 24:23), intends to do something (2 Chronicles 6:7), devoted to seeking the Lord (1 Chronicles 22:19), one that decides (2 Chronicles 6:7), desires to receive from the Lord (Psalm 21:1,2), turned to God's statutes (Psalm 119:36), and the heart that wants to do something (Romans 10:1).

All these scriptures point out the need to examine the "soil" of our heart.

Matthew 13:18-23, Mark 4:13-20, and Luke 8:4-15,

repeat what Jesus had to say about soil in our lives.

There are **hardened** areas. The soil has compacted because people and events have "walked" over us. Our hearts have become calloused. The seeds of God's word cannot take root. "Birds of indifference" can snatch away the seeds. What our eyes see (TV, movies, books, magazines, the internet) manipulate our senses and our choices.

Hebrews 3:7-8 begins with a warning about hardened hearts, encouraging believers to be faithful to God's voice, heeding His word and (:13) "encouraging one another daily – so that none of you may be hardened by sin's deceitfulness." Continue reading after Hebrews 3:12, through 4:2, and verse 7, to be instructed about a hardened heart.

Have you ever thought about what God's music sounds like: surf, waterfalls, bubbling streams, wind in the trees, bird's songs, the sound of gentle rain, frogs croaking, insects buzzing, a child's laughter, someone's whistle, the cry of a newborn baby, a distant train whistle? The world's music can pervert; God's music uplifts and gives peace.

Glaphre, *When The Pieces Don't Fit*, prayed, "Thank you God, for not letting me get away with a bad attitude. I was learning that each excuse I give for un-Christlike behavior makes the next excuse easier, and the soil in my heart's garden hardens more against receiving God's Word or hearing His voice."

We pursue pleasure rather than the Lord and His excellence in our lives. Personal ambitions are more important than using our gifts to minister for Him. All these things can become idols to harden us.

What about our thought life? Grudges, grievances, hostilities, bitterness?

I liken the story of Lot's wife looking back, to

ruminating over the past, bringing up hurts, slights, and deceptions. It turns us to "salt" and makes us unfruitful. The Lord cannot plant in that kind of soil. Soil which is heavy with salt (like the Dead Sea) will grow nothing. (You can pour salt over weeds growing in the cracks of your sidewalk and the weeds will never grow there again!)

A hardened soil in my life keeps God's seeds from growing.

Matthew 13:20 describes **rocky** soil. The rocks represent sin.

Many years ago, when I was a much younger Christian, someone gave me some instruction which has meant a lot to me and has repeatedly come back to me over time. This person said that since the Spirit of God had been flowing through me so fluently it had washed up to the surface some of the rocky places that I could not see before; "they were covered over with sand."

This person went on to say, "Now the Lord is instructing you to take these stones of offense and build them into a wall, and each shall represent to you an area in which the grace of God has moved.

"So do not stand back now and say, 'God, I see all these things in my life. How could You have chosen me, and how could You be wanting Your river to flow through me?'

"Bring every stone you find to Me, and say, 'Lord, here is another stone that has washed up to the surface.' You can now rejoice that the sinking sands are washing out of your life, and that the rocky places are appearing. Beneath the rocky places is that good, fertile soil that will bring forth a hundredfold.

"Gather the stones. Bring them to Me now, and I will use them in a wall that I will build around your spiritual vineyard. And that which was an offense to you will become a cornerstone of defense to you as you see the

Lord overcomes all weaknesses of the flesh, and weaknesses of the spirit, and weaknesses of the thoughts of the mind. And then the Lord shall establish you in the grace where you stand.

"Now you shall see the water flowing to wash away all the sandy soil, and you shall labor together with God to gather up all the stones out of the ground that remain. And the seed shall be sown.

"What is the chaff to the wheat in the day of the harvest? What will the stones that were taken away be to the harvesters? They will look on them and say, 'What is this?' And none shall remember the stony places, but all shall remember that fruitful field that brought forth a hundredfold.

"So do not become preoccupied with stones in your life, but keep your mind on the finished work. He who has begun this work will finish it. (Philippians 1:6)."

The Matthew 13 text describes **shallow** soil which has very little soil for a seed to sprout and grow. There is not enough room for the roots to grow and produce a healthy long-lived plant with fruit.

Because there is no depth of soil, there is limited nutrition for the plant to receive. That kind of soil will also not hold water. The stresses and strains of life beat like hot scorching sun on our "plant" life, and we will wilt and die. We have potential and promise, but there is nothing deep enough in our spirit to sustain us during trials and testings. We are not rooted and grounded in Christ, our Sustainer. We really don't know (or just don't believe) His Word.

We've been taught to be self-reliant, so we resist being God-dependent. He's our last resort, not our first contact. We put our trust in our church friends, pastor, fellowship; all the amenities which come from being a regular church attendant. These are necessary, but are a shallow substitute for a close relationship with Christ.

People and institutions will fail, but Christ will never fail. (Hebrews 13:5, Matthew 28:20) We need to recognize our stubborn resistance to God's ways and allow Him to remove these offensive stones and reveal a fertile soil where He can plant His seeds.

All soils are different. Applied spiritually, and in context with the practical application, we recognize that some spiritual soils have deficiencies; some minor, some deep-seated and in need of counseling.

How do we know what the problems are? We learn the general characteristics of our soil, making careful note of how plants perform in our garden. The Bible instructs us to examine ourselves. (1 Corinthians 11:28, 31) This is in the context of receiving communion. When we take into ourselves the blood and body of the Lord, earnestly asking Him to reveal our sins and shortcomings, and comparing them to the Word, He prescribes the necessary amendments for change, through the Holy Spirit who resides inside us.

Jeremiah 4:3 and Hosea 10:12 speak about breaking up **fallow ground**. This is idle, uncultivated, unproductive ground. Thorns (weeds) have to come out to make it ready to receive the Word of God and produce righteousness instead of sin.

Dake's Annotated Reference Bible, Dake Bible Sales, Inc., commentary states, "Each man must break up the fallow ground of his own life. Fallow ground is that which has been plowed but not sown; ground not in use; idle, crusted over and hardened until it needs to be broken up again to receive the seed." When was the last time you were truly broken before the Lord? Our hearts and wills must be broken and yielded to God. We must make ourselves willing to receive the Word of God and obey it; or seeking Him will not help us.

Dake continues, "Plow, disc, fertilize from the Word,

prepare for seed, water with tears. Watch your soil bring forth."

Do you have fallow ground of unused talents, or ministry abilities not being exercised?

The Matthew text continues, explaining **thorny and weedy** soil.

One day I wrote in my journal, "This morning I threw away some old pantyhose and shoes, and an old, dilapidated leather case which used to hold a nail file, tweezers, and cuticle scissors. I've had the leather case for so many years the stitching had broken and those items wouldn't stay in. The case was empty in my drawer.

"The Holy Spirit began to deal with my spirit about the old things we hang on to in our spiritual lives: hypocrisy, selfishness, bitterness, suspicion, pride, unforgiveness, jealousy, rejection, criticism, respecter-of-persons, lust, lying, fear, anger, anxiety, worry, unbelief, gossip, religious spirits, cursing, impatience, just to name a few. Pull out those weeds! These old ways become habits which are so much a part of what makes up our uniqueness that we're unwilling to let them go, even though they cause us (and others) pain and limit us from receiving God's best. (We excuse them by saying, 'Oh, that's just the way I'm wired!') They are part of the old man the Word instructs us to get rid of. (Ephesians 4:21-32) He has so much for us that's better, but until we have discarded the old, we won't need the new.

"I have the money to purchase a new case, more pantyhose and shoes, but as long as I 'make do' with what I have, I will not have anything better. I'll never have the character which better personifies the Lord."

Hebrews 6:7,8 cautions, "Land that drinks in the rain often falling on It, and that produces a crop useful to those for whom it is farmed, receives the blessing of God. But land that produces thorns and thistles is worthless and is in danger of being cursed. In the end it will be burned."

When your garden is full of beautiful flowers, there is no room for weeds to grow.

The best kind of soil to have in your spiritual garden is **loamy** (that's the kind of soil described in the first part of the Hebrews 6 scripture described above). It drains well, has sufficient organic matter to nourish the plants, and is soft enough for roots to go deep. With this kind of soil in our spiritual garden, problems cannot weigh us down. We know and believe God's Word and allow Him to guide us with it. It speaks to our spirit in every situation. Our roots are well-established in our relationship with the Lord, and our past has been a great teacher and strengthener, because we can see how the Lord has worked, using every situation and circumstance to enrich our spiritual soil.

One of the homes Ted and I bought was newly built. The developer had removed all the good topsoil and left only hard-as-rock decomposed granite. When Ted was attempting to put up cross-fencing, he had to use a chip bar to make holes for fence posts. Putting in flower beds was out of the question, and we found all kinds of construction debris which had to be removed from that soil.

Any time we allow the Spirit to dig around in our spiritual soil, there will be "construction" debris as God chips away at the creation He's building. These may be the world's ideas about life. There may be "produce" we have reaped from seeds of past mistakes. And then, there are those wrong attitudes!

So Ted and I added mushroom compost and compost available at the regional dump, and after the grass had been planted, we put all the clippings on the bed areas. It broke up that hard soil. In a few years I could push a shovel in very easily, and I soon found all kinds of earthworms working in that soil to digest the organic matter and keep the soil rich and easily worked.

God's Word is the perfect fertilizer we need in our spiritual soil. We can't get too much. Our soil will be rich and ready to produce good fruit. Psalm 119:11 says the Word keeps us from sin. Psalm 119:105 describes it as our light and our lamp. Psalm 107:20 states that it heals. Proverbs 30:5 calls it pure. And Hebrews 4:12 describes it as quick, sharp, powerful, and says that it divides.

After your garden soil has been analyzed to find what additives it needs, and after we add them, we till it, stir it up, and make it loose. The seeds can easily take root. Plant roots go deep, and there's nutrition for good growth. At this point, we must never walk on the soil and pack it down. (It's easier if we make our flower beds less than 4 feet across so we can reach in to work in it without having to walk on it.) We must apply that principle to our spiritual soil, as well. We should never let anything but the Lord's Spirit "walk" in our garden. He knows how to keep the soil productive. We should never allow the old attitudes, etc. to come back.

An ancient saying is, "The finest fertilizer on a gardener's ground is his own footprints; no strangers, no outsiders. Christ only should be walking in my garden." Don't admit "strangers" of any negative or faithless thoughts into your life.

George D. Scarseth has stated, "Productive soils and a people at peace fit together, each nourishing the other. Only well-nourished people can think of and serve others.

"An empty soil cannot support or give rise to a high civilization and culture. An empty soil cannot support a society so that it can look after its health. An empty soil is like a dead battery. From where shall the spark come for a new charge?!"

Rick Warren, *The Purpose Driven Life*, "It is not

enough just to believe the Bible: I must fill my mind with it so that the Holy Spirit can transform me with the truth. There are five ways to do this. You can receive it, read it, research it, remember it, and reflect on it.

"—you *receive* God's Word when you listen and accept it with an open, receptive attitude. The parable of the sower illustrates how our receptiveness determines whether or not God's Word takes root in our lives and bears fruit. Jesus identified three unreceptive attitudes–a closed mind (hard soil), a superficial mind (shallow soil), and a distracted mind (soil with weeds) –and then He said, *Consider carefully how you listen.* Daily Bible reading will keep you in range of God's voice."

An Irish blessing: "May there always be work for your hands to do. May your purse always hold a coin or two. May the sun always shine on your windowpane. May a rainbow be certain to follow each rain. May the hand of a friend always be near you. May God fill your heart with gladness to cheer you."

Notes

THE TEST OF MY LIFE'S SOIL

Scriptures from NIV and NKJ.

Lamentations 3:40. Let us examine our ways and test them, and let us return to the Lord.

2 Corinthians 13:5. Examine yourselves to see whether you are in the faith, test yourselves. Do you not realize that Christ Jesus is in you - unless, of course, you fail the test?

An intelligent person recognizes they are engaging in self-defeating behavior.

Self-examination is painful and uncomfortable, and often is inconvenient. We'd rather not look inward.

---

1. If I die tonight will my soul be in Heaven or Hell tomorrow morning?

> (John 1:12-13) "For as many as received Him to them He gave the right to become children of God, to those who believe in His name, who were born, not of blood, nor of the will of the flesh, nor of the will of man, but of God." (John 5:24.) " Most assuredly, I say to you, he who hears My word and believes in Him who sent Me has everlasting life, and shall not come into judgment, but has passed from death unto life."

2. What draws me away from the Lord?

> (James 1:13-14) "When tempted, no one should say, 'God is tempting me.' For God cannot be tempted by evil, nor does He tempt anyone, but each one is tempted when, by

his own evil desire, he is dragged away and enticed."

3. What kind of "rocks" are in the soil of my life?

(Matthew 13:5-6, 20-21) Verse 5 "(seed) Fell on rocky places, where it did not have much soil. It sprang up quickly, because the soil was shallow. But when the sun came up the plants were scorched, and they withered because they had no root." Verse 20-21 "The one who received the seed that fell on rocky places is the man who hears the word and at once receives it with joy. But since he has no root, he lasts only a short time. When trouble or persecution comes because of the word, he quickly falls away."

4. Am I committed to the Lord: heart, mind, and soul?

(1 Samuel 7:3) "And Samuel said to the whole house of Israel, 'If you are returning to the Lord with all our hearts, then rid yourselves of the foreign gods and the Ashtoreths and commit yourselves to the Lord and serve Him only, and He will deliver you out of the hand of the Philistines."

(1 Peter 3:15) "But in your hearts set apart Christ as Lord, always be prepared to give an account for the hope that is within you."

5. Am I concerned that I may grieve the Holy Spirit by my attitude, my words, my actions?

Ephesians 4, 5 and 6 (whole chapters)

6. Is Christ the Lord of my life? (As Thomas declared in John 20:28). Read John 20:24-31; especially notice verse 31.

7. Has anyone noticed a difference in me since I committed my life to the Lord? Do I see a change?

> (2 Corinthians 3:18) "And we, who with unveiled faces all reflect the Lord's glory, are becoming transformed into His likeness with ever-increasing glory which comes from the Lord, Who is the Spirit."

> (Ephesians 5:1-2) "Be imitators of God, therefore, as dearly loved children, and live a life of love, just as Christ loved us and gave Himself up for us, as a fragrant offering and sacrifice to God."

8. Do I crumble, panic, or get offended when problems arise?

> (Psalm 119:165) "Great peace have they who love Your law, and nothing can make them stumble (or nothing shall offend them)."

> (Luke 12:22-31) "Then Jesus said to His disciples: 'Therefore I tell you, do not worry about your life, what you will eat; or about your body, what you shall wear. Life is more than food, and the body more than clothes. Consider the ravens: they do not sow or reap, they have no storeroom or barn; yet God

feeds them. And how much more valuable you are than birds? Who of you by worrying can add a single hour to his life? Since you cannot do this very little thing, why do you worry about the rest? Consider how the lilies grow. They do not labor or spin. Yet I tell you not even Solomon in all his splendor was dressed like one of these. If that is how God clothes the grass of the field, which is here today, and tomorrow is thrown into the fire, how much more will He clothe you, O you of little faith? And do not set your heart on what you will eat or drink; do not worry about it. For the pagan world runs after all such things, and your Father knows that you need them. But seek His kingdom, and these things will be given to you as well.'"

(James 1:2-4) "Consider it pure joy, my brothers, whenever you face trials of many kinds, because you know that the testing of your faith develops perseverance. Perseverance must finish its work so that you may be mature and complete, not lacking anything."

(John 16:33) "I have told you these things, so that in Me you will have peace. In this world you will have trouble, but take heart! I have overcome the world."

9. Does my mouth show what is in my heart?

(Matthew 12:33-37) "Make a tree good and its fruit will be good, or make a tree bad and its fruit will be bad, for a tree is recognized by its fruit. You brood of vipers (religious leaders) how can you who are evil say anything good? For out of the overflow of the heart the mouth speaks. The good man brings good things out of the good stored up in him, and the evil man brings evil things out of the evil stored up in him. But I tell you that men will have to give account on the day of judgment for every careless word they have spoken. For by your words you will be acquitted, and by your words you will be condemned."

(Ephesians 4:29) "Do not let any unwholesome talk come out of your mouths, but only what is helpful for building others up according to their needs, that it may benefit those who listen."

(James 1:26) "If anyone considers himself religious and yet does not keep a tight rein on his tongue, he deceives himself and his religion is worthless."

(James 2:12-13) "Speak and act as those who are going to be judged by the law that gives freedom because judgment without mercy will be shown to anyone who has not been merciful. Mercy triumphs over judgment."

10. Do I consider myself to be hot, cold, or lukewarm (in my walk with the Lord)?

(Revelation 3:15-16) "I know your deeds, that you are neither cold nor hot. I wish you were either one or the other! So because you are lukewarm – neither hot nor cold – I am about to spit you out of My mouth."

11. Do I serve the Lord with a glad heart by serving others? (Not just with money.)

(Galatians 5:13b) "Serve one another in love."

(Colossians 3:23) "Whatsoever you do, do it heartily as unto the Lord."

(1 Peter 4:9-10) "Be hospitable to one another without grumbling. As each one has received a gift, minister it to one another, as good students of the manifold grace of God."

12. Am I determined to obey and practice the Word no matter what it costs?

(James 1:22-25) "Do not merely listen to the word, and so deceive yourselves. Do what it says. Anyone who listens to the word but does not do what it says is like a man who looks at his face in a mirror and after looking at himself, goes away and immediately forgets what he looks like. But the man who looks intently into the perfect law that gives freedom, and continues to do this, not forgetting what he has heard, but doing it - he will be blessed in what he does."

13. Do I pay tithes and offerings?

(Malachi 3:8-10) "Will a man rob God? Yet you rob Me. But you ask, 'How do we rob You?' In tithes and offerings."

14. Are there things, or people, I love more than the Lord?

(1 John 2:15-17) "Do not love the world or anything in the world. If anyone loves the world, the love of the Father is not in him. For everything in the world–the cravings of sinful man, the lust of his eyes and the boasting of what he has and does – comes not from the Father but from the world. The world and its desires pass away, but the man who does the will of God lives forever."

15. Are prayer and Bible study an important part of my life?

(Luke 18:1) "Then Jesus told His disciples a parable to show them that they should always pray and not give up."

(Romans 12:12) "Be joyful in hope, patient in affliction, faithful in prayer."

(Philippians 4:6) "Do not be anxious about anything, but in everything by prayer and petition, with thanksgiving, present your requests to God."

(Colossians 4:2) "Devote yourselves to

prayer, being watchful and thankful."

16. Am I concerned about the salvation of my relatives and friends; the people of the world?

> (Mark 16:15) He said to them, "Go into all the world and preach the good news to all creation."

17. Do I hold grudges or refuse to forgive others when they "walk" on my heart?

> (Ephesians 4:32) "Be kind and compassionate to one another, forgiving each other, just as in Christ God forgave you."

18. If I was accused of being a Christian, is there enough evidence to convict me?

> (2 Peter 3:14) "So then, dear friends, since you are looking forward to this, make every effort to be found spotless, blameless, and at peace with Him."

> (1 Thessalonians 5:23-24) "May God Himself, the God of peace, sanctify you through and through. May your whole spirit, soul, and body be kept blameless at the coming of our Lord Jesus Christ. The One who calls you is faithful, and He will do it."

Notes

CHAPTER TWO

WHAT'S GROWING IN MY GARDEN?

Source: *Sunset Western Garden Book*, Lane Publishing Company, Menlo Park, CA.
Country Living magazine, August 1996.
"Biennial Bliss," Rebecca Sawyer-Fay

Where you live (your climate zone) will determine what kind of plants will grow best. Plants differ immensely in their response to different climates. Many cannot live through a cold winter; others need it. Some cannot perform well in coastal humidity; others depend on the damp air.

A plant climate zone is an area in which a common set of temperature ranges, humidity patterns, and other geographic and seasonal characteristics allow certain plants to succeed and others to fail.

Remember, there's a difference between weather and climate. Weather is what's going on in the atmosphere outside your window. Climate is the accumulation of weather effects in your area throughout the cycle of seasons.

Some important factors which make up a climate zone are the distance from the equator, the temperatures during the winter, the hours of daylight, increases and decreases in temperature during the seasons, elevation, the influence of oceans, amount of rainfall, and the influence of continental air mass. Mountains and hills and local terrain can also be factors.

Conditions in your garden can create micro-climates, like a solid fence or row of trees which trap colder air. A south facing wall will accumulate heat. There are also thermal belts, hilltops, swales, canyons, and fog belts.

Plant life begins with a seed which puts down roots. Each seed, as large as a sunflower seed, or as small as dust (a begonia seed), stores enough food to sustain a new plant until it is capable of manufacturing its own food. This food is in the form of sugar which the plant converts into starch, depending on the season. Some seeds are bulbs, tubers, corms, or rhizomes. All the possibilities, capabilities, and characteristics for what the seed will become are stored in it, regardless of its size.

Germination requires proper environmental conditions: moisture, oxygen, favorable temperature, and sometimes light (some seeds require more, some less). Seeds from many temperate climate plants must be dormant (sleeping) for a time. This prevents them from being killed by winter after they germinate. Some seeds remain dormant for many years.

Some seeds are dormant because of a hard seed coat impermeable to water. Germination can be stimulated by soaking in water, nicking with a file, or rubbing on coarse sandpaper. (The morning glory is one of these.) Others need cold, fire, or acid.

I read an article about controlled burns written by a biologist at the Forest Service's Southern Region office in Atlanta. He said the scientific advances of the past 15 to 20 years support controlled burns. He was quoted saying, "(A number of plant) species are in danger of getting eliminated unless we put fire back on the southern Appalachians."

And the head of the Southern Region's fire program said (in the same article), "Table mountain pine, pitch pine, short leaf pine, and oak are some tree species which depend on fire. Cones of the table mountain pine will not open unless they are heated."

Plants store energy from light (photosynthesis). If light is withheld long enough, the plant dies. All plant life relies on it. (Pho means put together with light.)

A stem shoots up, acting like a straw, to pass nourishment which the roots take from the soil up to the leaves. It also returns the sugar manufactured in the leaves to the roots. The stem supports the plant and stores food which feeds the plant during dormancy, to start growth in the spring, and to help the seeds develop. The cadmium layer (outer bark) on a tree is the "straw" and if it is completely cut around, the tree will die. (That's why it's so important to use trimmers with care.)

As soon as the true leaves open to the sun, the plant gets down to work as a complete organism. (Notice the first set of leaves which appear after planting marigolds. They are rounded on the end. These are not the true leaves. The next set of leaves will be uneven in design and are the true marigold leaves.)

Sunlight strikes the leaves, and through the action of green matter known as chlorophyll, chemical substances drawn from the air and the soil are converted to food. This explains why seedlings should not be transplanted when their first leaves appear; their roots are not yet established. This also explains why the plant needs richer soil – either in a transplant flat or the garden – after its true leaves appear: the leaves have gone into action and have put the roots to work, drawing nutrients from the soil.

The top side of most leaves do the work of converting raw materials to food. The bottom have minute breathing pores which open and close to release excess water vapor and oxygen and to admit carbon dioxide. At night, these openings expel the extra carbon dioxide which has not been used during the daylight hours. The pores close when the weather is dry, open when it is moist.

Leaves vary in size, shape, and intensity of green color according to the plant's need for sunlight. This is why large-leafed plants are usually at home in shade, where their large area of chlorophyll draws the utmost from the reduced supply of sunlight. At the other extreme, desert plants usually have small, grayish leaves which are adapted to the merciless exposure to the sun.

All plants have flowers; some are barely noticeable. Most flowers, a means for reproducing the plant, have both male and female parts. Bees help in pollination, moving pollen from the stamen (male) to the pistils (female) which has an ovary. If both sexes are not on the plant, then you will need a pair of plants to reproduce; usually of a different species of the same plant. This is often true in fruit trees, blueberries, and is true of corn, for example.

I don't know who authored the article, "*God Made Life Interesting,"* but it was a handout in one of my classes. The article said, "Seeds may be dropped into the ground upside down or sideways, yet the plants come up to the surface. (This is especially true in most bulbs.) One grain of corn will produce a stalk on which there may be two ears, with perhaps 742 grains on each ear. A light crop of wheat will produce approximately thirty grains on each stalk; a good crop of wheat will produce approximately sixty grains on each stalk. There will always be an even number of grains.

> "Beans grow up a pole from left to right, while the morning glory grows up a pole from right to left. If turned upside down, 'twining' plants will uncoil and re-circle their support. Guide a twiner in the 'wrong' direction, and the plant will rewind itself. The higher a twiner grows, the more tightly it claps its support.

"The dandelion will grow above its surroundings whether the grass be two, ten, or twenty inches (after 24 inches the weight of the flower causes the stalk to bend) for it must get up into the sunlight. An ordinary watermelon will have ten stripes on it. Larger ones may have twelve to sixteen stripes, but always an even number.

"Every form of life in the vegetable and animal kingdom has a predetermined set of characteristics, a master plan, perfect in every detail . . .God's plan. God has a perfect plan for my life and yours which supplies all our needs. HIS WORD (2 Peter 1:3). By His grace we receive strength to rise above all our circumstances. (Romans 8:31).

"How wonderful to witness His majesty in the changing seasons!"

Annuals grow one year, go to seed, and die. If possible, collect their seeds and plant them next year. Marigold, zinnia, and sunflowers have seeds which are easy to collect. Be sure they are very dry on the plant before picking them and store them in a dry container in a cool place, tightly covered. The refrigerator is a good place.

Perennials are plants which grow permanently for more than two years. Some (like peonies) are forever! Most bulbs would be considered perennial.

Biennials, by definition, produce only vegetative growth their first year, then flower and complete their life cycle the second year. Although some, such as hollyhocks, may put on a repeat performance the third year, blossoms are often inferior and plants less vigorous. Hollyhocks and several other biennials freely self-sow, however, they may prove as long-lived as any perennial. They can naturalize and endure for generations. Foxgloves, too, are beloved for their tenacity, returning year after year to lightly shaded beds and borders. Canterbury bells, English daisy, Forget-me-not, Pansy, Honesty or money plant, and Sweet William, are some very reliable biennials.

Labels on plants purchased at a reputable nursery will indicate the amount of sun needed for maximum performance. Full sun is 6-8 hours a day. Partial sun is 4 hours a day. Partial shade is two or less hours a day. Filtered sun and broken shade is under trees or arbors. Heavy shade is no sun. Morning sun is much less intense than evening. Some plants will tolerate full morning sun but wilt under afternoon sun. Hydrangeas, peonies and hostas are examples of plants which will grow best with morning sun only. (In summer, here in East Tennessee, even morning sun can be quite intense. I found it necessary to protect a young hydrangea bush with a large umbrella until the sun moved around to the south. Now that the bush is a few years older, when it starts to wilt I give it a drink at the roots, which perks it up. I do not water the leaves because the water can act like a magnifying glass and burn them.)

Another interesting fact, author unknown:

> "Although mistletoe adorns many a door frame during the holidays, it's a strange plant to have evolved into a symbol of amorous affection. Mistletoe is a flowering perennial plant that grows as a parasite on woody trees and shrubs. Although some species have berries that can propel their sticky seeds for some distance, it most often happens that birds ingest the berries and then expel the

seeds through their digestive tract in fecal matter. Because the birds are frequently perched on tree branches, the seeds germinate there and penetrate the host tree or shrub. Thus, the name 'mistletoe' is derived from the method of seed dispersal. The Anglo-Saxon word 'mistle' means dung, and 'tan' means twig. Literally translated, mistletoe means, 'Dung on a twig!'

"How did a plant with such a lowly growing habit become a symbol of romance? Perhaps it's related to the fact that it's a parasitic plant that's dependent on the hospitality of another. Regardless of how you read it, the mistletoe's current reputation is a composite of a variety of culturally specific meanings. Druids regarded it as sacred, an aphrodisiac that could bestow life and fertility, and capable of protecting one against poison. Mistletoe's reputation as a sexual charm and fertility symbol evolved in England, Greece, and Scandinavia. In some parts of England, Christmas mistletoe is burned on the twelfth night, in case the boys and girls who kissed under it never marry.

"Current mistletoe etiquette says that a person should pluck a berry from the mistletoe branch every time they kiss under it. When no more berries remain on the plant, there should be no more kissing."

Reader's Digest, *North American Wildlife*, 1982, has an interesting bit of information about the cattail.

> "One need never starve where cattails grow. In fall and winter, the starchy rhizomes can be peeled and cooked like potatoes or dried and pounded into flour. The dormant sprouts that grow from them are tastiest steamed, a dish known as Russian asparagus. In spring and early summer, the young shoots can be eaten raw or cooked, and the immature flower spikes can be boiled and eaten like miniature ears of corn. Later on, the abundant pollen produced by the male flowers that make up the top half of the flowering spike can be used without grinding as a fine-textured flour. The leaves are not edible, but they have been woven into mats, chair seats, baskets and even roofs. The fluffy white fruits have been used to stuff pillows, and campers have found them a good emergency replacement for down in sleeping bags and jackets."

Garden Gate magazine, in its June 2002 issue (No. 45), printed an excellent article, "**Gather Seeds, - get a head start on next year's garden**," authored by Anne Nieland.

> "One of the fascinating things about gardening is seeds. Whether you buy them in a paper envelope or your plants toss out offspring on their own, seeds are nature's little wonders. All that's needed to grow an entire plant is stored in a tiny seed. Besides that, they're easy to transport so you can share them. Many are relatively easy to start, too. With a combination of water, soil and

sunlight, your garden is ready to grow.

"Getting started.

Wherever there is–or was–a bloom, there's the potential for collecting seeds. Each spent flower is a small puzzle. The key is figuring out where the seeds are so you can collect them. Some are easy to gather, such as marigold. This plant all but hands you a neat packet of seeds that you can separate from the rest of the flower. Flowing tobacco seeds are just as easy to collect. The flower petals fall out of small, upright cups. When these cups are dry, just pour the seeds into your container.

"Others, such as touch-me-not and partridge pea, burst out of their pods. Unless you sit in a lawn chair and keep a close watch, you won't know exactly when the seeds pop. You can still collect from these plants, but you'll have to outsmart them. One way to catch the bursting seeds is to tie a bag over the dying flowers with string or twist ties. Be sure to use something that breathes, such as a paper or muslin bag or a nylon stocking, so the seeds can continue to mature on the plant. Check the bag after a few days to see what popped in your absence.

"When you're choosing a plant to collect from, concentrate your efforts on plants that aren't hybrids. Hybrlds are plants that were bred from two separate, but related, species to produce a third variety. The seeds from hybrids, if they're produced at all, will revert back to one of the original plants and be different from the plant you grew. Usually hybrids are marked as such on the plant tag or seed packet. Seeds from heirloom or open-pollinated varieties will come true. They'll grow into plants that look like the generations before them. Choose seeds from several plants if you can. That way you'll have more genetic diversity in your garden.

"And be sure that you collect from the healthiest plants, since some diseases can be carried into the next generation in or on a seed. First, check the seed heads. Steer clear of those with insects. Then look at the leaves. If you notice any yellowing or gnarled foliage, choose a different plant.

"Mature seeds only, please–Whatever you collect, you want to be sure that the seeds are fully mature before you harvest them – immature seeds won't sprout. There are a few clues to tell if the seeds are ready. Usually they'll turn a darker color than the rest of the plant. The capsule holding the seed can dry to a different color, as well. Still not sure how to tell? Just leave the flower or pod on the plant until it has dried on its own. It's okay to snip the entire pod at this point. Many plants give you several opportunities to collect seeds.

Be sure to write down the date, name of the plant, and where you collected the seeds.

That way you can go back later to identify the plant if you need to.

Drying your collection – Though your seeds may look and feel dry, it's likely that they still contain enough moisture that they'll spoil in storage. They'll need to be dried. To give your seeds a head start, collect them when the weather is dry, such as on a sunny afternoon.

"Lay freshly collected loose seeds, pods, or seed heads on paper towels placed in a warm, dry location. Keep them out of direct sun, which can cause them to degrade. If you've harvested flower heads still on the stems you can hang them upside down. If you need to, place a paper or muslin sack over the seed heads to keep free spirited seeds from dropping away.

"Depending on the humidity, it should take a few days to a couple of weeks for the seeds to dry. Here's a quick way to check if they're dry enough: Place the seeds in an airtight glass container at room temperature. If you see condensation inside after a few hours, they need more drying time.

"**Separating the seed from the chaff.** Once they're dry, your seeds may still be inside their pods. The seeds are easier to store and less likely to rot if there's no chaff– the dry flower parts surrounding the seed. So thresh and winnow, and you'll have clean seeds ready to store.

"Threshing separates the seed from what's holding it. This can be as simple as using your hands to crack seed pods. If you need more direct force to separate the seed from the flower parts, try rubbing the seeds between two boards. This works well with purple coneflowers or any other flowers with stubborn, seed-holding capsules. Sometimes you'll need a more efficient way to thresh a lot of seeds. Beating a pillowcase full of seed pods against a table is a good way to thresh the large number of collected seeds.

"Once you've threshed, it's likely you'll need to winnow, or remove the loosened chaff from the seeds. Using a fan to blow the chaff from the seeds is one way; or put the seeds and chaff in a bag and shake it up. Like magic, they'll often sort themselves.

"Some seeds, such as large zinnias, are about the same size and shape as their chaff, so these winnowing techniques won't work. You can pick out the seeds with a tweezers, or leave the chaff mixed in. Just make sure that the seed-chaff mix is dry so you don't have to worry about the seeds rotting. The disadvantage is that the mix takes up more storage space, and you may have to guess at how thickly you're planting in spring.

"**A seed saved is a plant earned.** Once

your seeds are cleaned, the next step is to store them so they stay viable. That's just a term meaning your seeds are alive. Even though they may seem like little more than grains of sand, seeds are living organisms. They're just dormant, or resting, until you give them the okay to sprout by planting them.

"But just because they're dormant doesn't mean they don't need a little TLC. To keep your seeds fresh, remember these three words: cool, dark, and dry.

"Properly sealed in airtight containers after drying, most seeds store best at 40 to 45 degrees. Check around for a cool spot far from heat sources, such as the furnace. Storing your seeds where it's dark will also help preserve their viability. This can be as simple as placing all your bags or jars in a cardboard box or a brown paper sack.

"As a rule, store seeds at 25 to 35 percent humidity. Do this by sealing your dried seeds in airtight glass or metal containers, like jelly jars or resealable bags; empty film containers work well too.

"Freezing is a great way to store seeds for a few years. But before you freeze seeds, you need to dry them even more than usual. Otherwise they can die when ice crystals form inside them. So first, reduce the moisture to 6 to 8 percent using color-indicating silica gel, a desiccant. Make a mix of half silica crystals and half seeds in an airtight container. Leave it until the silica changes to pink–about a week. Then remove the seeds and store them in an airtight container. Hint: Keep smaller seeds separate from the silica by wrapping them in a coffee filter so you can find them again easily.

"Testing, one, two, three– Last year I found a package of lettuce seeds that was 10 years old. I tossed them out in my garden–and was surprised to be harvesting salad a few weeks later. Now, I don't recommend holding on to your seeds for a decade, or even a few years–you'll have a better success rate with fresher seeds. But how can you tell how well they'll grow? Check their viability with a germination test. Here's what you do: scatter 10 seeds on a wet paper towel, roll it up and seal it in a resealable plastic bag. Set the bag in a warm location, such as on the top of the refrigerator. After three days, unroll the paper towel and count the seeds that sprouted. Divide that number into 10, and you'll have your percent germination.

"Because some seeds germinate sporadically, give them a few extra days. However, after about six days, seeds can rot, so don't hold them longer than that.

"Your percent germination will tell you how thickly to plant. Purchased seeds usually have a germination rate of 90 percent or more. Rates as low as 30 to 40 percent are still worth planting, but sow them about twice as thick.

"Once you start collecting, it can be habit forming! If you collect more seeds than you need, trying using seed exchanges to share and trade. On the internet, www.gardenweb.com is one of the more active venues I've found.

"Start by gathering from a few plants to supplement what you buy. That way you can test drive your collected seeds and have some to share. As your plants bloom and fade, don't look at it as the end. It's really the beginning of next year's garden."

And finally, another way to multiply your plants (or those from friends) is take cuttings, as instructed in the following article **"Don't buy new plants, just clone old ones,"** by Kent Steinriede of Gannett News Service.

"When homeowners need new plants, they often turn to just two sources: seeds or the garden center. But there's another way to fill your garden with new plants, for free. Clone them.

"The simplest way to clone a plant is to take a cutting, dip it in growth hormone powder and put the stem in a growing medium, such as peat moss, seed-starting soil or perlite stones, and wait for roots to grow.

"Most cuttings root easily. Every plant is different. Many houseplants, ivy, geraniums, and tropicals, such as impatiens and coleus, can easily be propagated in a glass of water, so long as you keep the glass topped off with water. Jade plant cuttings root easily in soil, but the cutting needs to dry out and scab over for at least 48 hours before planting.

"How long it takes to grow roots depends on the plant, available moisture to the cutting, and the medium in which you plant the cutting. Estimates range from two weeks for geraniums to more than six months for some trees. The easiest way to figure out if the cutting has grown roots is to give it a light tug. If there is resistance, you've got roots.

"At this point, the roots are very fragile. Don't pull the plant out of its rooting medium. Pour the medium out of the container and brush it away from the roots. Then plant the cutting in soil and keep it out of direct sunlight for about a week, which will allow it to harden and adjust to its new environment.

"Layer trees and shrubs. In most cases, this takes about a year, but the new plant is better nourished because it gets its sustenance from its parent the whole time the roots are forming.

"To create a new plant by layering, find a low branch that easily can touch the ground. With a wire coat hanger, make a staple large enough to hold down the branch. Cut a slice in the branch with a razor blade and brush the "tongue" that sticks out with rooting hormone powder. Bend the branch at the cut and use the staple to hold it down. Tie the rest of the stem to a small stake that will hold it vertical.

"Serpentine layering, in which the stem is cut and pegged down in several places is a good method for vines and climbers. This also takes about a year. The resulting plants should be potted and grown in a cold frame before they go outside.

"Finally, air layering works well with rubber trees and split-leaf philodendrons. Cut a tongue just below a leafy area. Brush the slit with rooting hormone. Then fill it with very moist sphagnum moss. Wrap the cut and moss with clear plastic. Seal it to the plant's stem with wire bread ties or tape. Check occasionally to make sure that the moss is still moist. When the roots are visible, clip the stalk below the moss and plant it, along with the moss, in soil."

SPIRITUAL APPLICATION

God's word is the seed for my soil.

People live in different climate zones with dissimilar "weather" conditions. This diversity includes married, never married, widowed, divorced with children and without, old, young, employed, unemployed, and retired. The "weather" is sometimes calm, sometimes stormy.

We all have problems with weeds in our garden: our tongues, anger, disobedience, thought life, lying, and unbelief, to name a few. These grow in every climate. They will get out of control and choke our garden's bed; our plants will be sickly, lack nourishment, and be stunted.

Jim Rohn was quoted as saying, "We must all wage an intense, lifelong battle against the constant downward pull. If we relax, the bugs and weeds of negativity will move into our garden and take away everything of value. You cannot take the mild approach to the weeds in your mental garden. You have got to hate weeds enough to kill them. Weeds are not something you handle – weeds are something you devastate."

Colossians 2:7 LB. "Since you have accepted Christ, live in vital union with Him. Let your roots grow down into Him and draw up nourishment from Him. See that you go on growing in the Lord."

Psalm 144:12a GNB. "May your sons in their youth be like plants that grow up strong."

Proverbs 4:20-24 GNB. "Pay attention to what I say. Listen to my words. Never let them get away from you. Remember them and keep them in your heart. They will give life and health to anyone who understands them. Be careful how you think; your life is shaped by your thoughts. Never say anything that isn't true. Have nothing to do with lies and misleading words."

1 Samuel 15:22-23 GNB. (What Samuel told Saul), "Which does the Lord prefer; obedience or offerings and sacrifices? It is better to obey Him than to sacrifice the best sheep to Him. Rebellion against Him is as bad as witchcraft, and arrogance is as sinful as idolatry."

Proverbs 14:29 GNB. "If you stay calm, you are wise, but if you have a hot temper, you only show how stupid you are."

Proverbs 15:1 GNB. "A gentle answer quiets anger, but a harsh one stirs it up."

Proverbs 14:30 NIV. "A heart at peace gives life to the body, but envy rots the bones."

The garden of my life has perennials; those which are continuing or enduring through many years; perpetual, everlasting, unceasing. That is my relationship with the Lord.

Prayer, Bible study, and fellowship are annuals which need replenishing often.

My garden has trees. Psalm 92:12-14 GNB. "The righteous will flourish like palm trees, they will grow like the cedars of Lebanon. They are like trees planted in the house of the Lord, that flourish in the Temple of our God, that still bear fruit in old age and are always green and strong."

There is a lawn and a water feature in my life's garden. Psalm 23:2 GNB. "He lets me rest in fields of green grass and leads me to quiet pools of fresh water."

A study conducted by the Human-Environment Research Laboratory at the University of Illinois at Urbana-Champaign has shown levels of aggression were significantly lower among people who had some kind of natural setting outside their apartments versus those who did not. Some scientists believe people living under the stress of crowding, high temperatures, and noise suffer from what they call 'chronic mental fatigue.' The result can be irritability and impulsive behavior, both important ingredients of aggressiveness. Exposure to green spaces, such as lawns or play areas shaded by trees, can reduce the negative effects of chronic mental fatigue.

Paths in my garden take me to places of rest and safety. Psalm 23:3b GNB. "He guides me in the right paths as He has promised." Isaiah 32:18 Amplified. "My people shall dwell in a peaceable habitation, in safe dwellings, and in quiet resting places."

My garden bears fruit. Galatians 5:22-23.

And there are birds, bees, and butterflies: people who flit in and out of my life. They provide beauty and music. I provide "water" and "food" for them. Some will build "nests" and raise young for a season. This is a sign that my garden is a place of nourishment.

A Gardener Looks at the Fruits of the Spirit, W. Phillip Keller, Word Books, states an excellent application for Galatians 5:22-23.

> "Like good seed introduced into good garden soil, it must come from a source outside the garden. It does not spring from the soil of our own souls and spirits spontaneously. Our human nature is not righteousness. (Jeremiah 17:9 and John 6:63) It is the spirit that quickens; the flesh (my human nature) profits nothing. The words that I speak to you are spirit, and they are life.
>
> "Love is selflessness. It is spelled out in 1 Corinthians 13:1-7. 'Does not seek its own, is not selfish, or self-centered. Does not rejoice in iniquity but rather rejoices in the truth. Not easily provoked, but is serene and stable. Suffers long, perseveres, is patient. Is merciful, thoughtful, concerned; it envies

not. Is gracious, generous, is kind and good. It thinks no evil but has faith in God and others. Is humble and gentle. Is disciplined and controlled.'

"Joy. Is not dependent upon people or circumstances. It springs from the presence of God in a person's life. Ephesians 3:20 LB. 'Now glory be to God Who by His mighty power at work within us is able to do far more than we would ever dare to ask or even dream of infinitely beyond our highest prayers, desires, thoughts, or hopes.'

"Peace. Is the selfless, self-giving, self-losing, self-forgetting, self-sacrificing love of God, despite all adversities of life. Romans 14:17, 'For the kingdom of God is not meat and drink, but righteousness and peace and joy in the Holy Ghost.' Philippians 4:6-8 GNB 'Don't worry about anything, but in all your prayers ask God for what you need, always asking Him with a thankful heart. And God's peace, which is far beyond human understanding, will keep your hearts and minds safe in union with Christ Jesus. Fill your minds with those things that are good and that deserve praise: things that are true, noble, right, pure, lovely, and honorable.'

"Patience. Is the powerful capacity of selfless love to suffer long under adversity and enables a man or woman to remain steadfast under strain, not standing still but pressing on. It is not weak or insipid, but is a force of enormous power and influence. Jesus told the parable (Matthew 18:23-33) of the man who owed an enormous debt and asked his creditor to be patient with him until he paid. We, on the other hand, want instant results and our piece of flesh.

"Kindness. A truly kind person does not flinch at the cost of extending kindness. Matthew 5:43-48 tells us to love our enemies, bless those that curse us, do good to those that hate us, pray for those who despise and persecute us. We no longer show love to get love back. No longer are we kind in order to be complemented and thought well of. We no longer give for what we can get.

"Goodness. It costs a great deal to be good! Jesus gave His life! It is a supernatural outgrowth of the life of Christ within; not forced or artificial, a simple expression of God's Spirit at work in me. I am not phony. I have no sense of pride or patronage toward others. I help the downtrodden. My goodness does not have to be publicized or paraded. Goodness is its own best advertisement.

"Faith. Hebrews. 12:2. 'Looking unto Jesus, the Author and Finisher of our faith.' When I am confident that Christ cares for me and loves me, I can quietly carry on, living in serenity, strength and stability. I am not shaken by the stormy events or unpredictable behavior of others around me. I give and give and give myself to God and others.

"Humility. Matthew 18:4 'Whosoever therefore shall humble himself as this little child, the same is greatest in the kingdom of heaven.' 1 Corinthians 13:4,5 'Love is not puffed up, does not behave unseemly, and seeks not her own.'

"Self-control. For the Christian, this means that my whole person, my whole being, body, soul, spirit, comes under the control of Christ. I am under authority. My will is the key area which Christ must come to control if I am to be of any consequence in His economy. My tongue is like a fire. It is a world of wrong, occupying its place in my body and spreading evil throughout my whole being. It sets on fire the entire course of my existence with the fire that comes to it from hell itself.

Man is able to tame and has tamed all other creatures–wild animals and birds, reptiles and fish. But no one has ever been able to tame the tongue. It is evil and uncontrollable, full of deadly poison. We use it to give thanks to our Lord and Father and also to curse our fellow man, who is created in the likeness of God. Words of thanksgiving and cursing pour out from the same mouth. No spring of water pours out sweet water and bitter water from the same opening."

Keller concludes, "Lest the reader be discouraged, let it be said here again that fruit production in our Christian experience, just as in an orchard or garden, is not something that goes on with great fanfare, noise or theatrics. From the opening of the first tiny bud under the impulse of spring sunshine, to the perfect ripening of the fully formed fruit beneath late Indian summer skies in fall, the whole process goes on quietly, serenely, and surely. It is the Spirit of God, who by His presence within, guarantees growth, maturity and conformity to Christ."

What pleases a gardener is the evidence (fruits or flowers) for all their work. What pleases our Heavenly Father is beauty and fruits of the Spirit in our lives. Proverbs 14:14 says you harvest what you plant, whether good or bad.

WORDS OF WISDOM

Henry Ward Beecher said, "Flowers are the sweetest things God ever made and forgot to put a soul into."

Anonymous. "It's said that life is like a patchwork, made of square snippets of time bound together by the stitches of memory."

While you are sleeping your brain is still active in dreams, and your body is still at work. Dormant plants/ trees are still actively growing, drawing nourishment and water through their roots. They will emerge in season.

Mary Jane Worden, *Virtue Magazine*, 9/10/91. "I am convinced that God has built into all of us an appreciation of beauty and has even allowed us to participate in the creation of beautiful things and places. It may be one way God brings healing to our brokenness, and a way that we can contribute toward bringing wholeness to our fallen world."

Contributed by my mom, "Unless the seed we sow is a good example, the fruit we bear will be sour grapes."

From a wall plaque: "Anyone can count the seeds in an apple, but only God can count the apples in a seed."

Women's Devotional New Testament, NIV, Zondervan. "Dandelions. No matter how carefully I try to pull one up, I never get the whole thing. The root stays deep in the ground, threatening to grow up and blossom again.

> "But despite their bad reputation, dandelions are pretty little flowers with their yellow strands all tucked neatly into the center. And truly they are the most beautiful of all flowers when presented clutched in a child's dirty little hand. No one gets yelled at for picking them. Perhaps they grow only to be used and enjoyed by children.
>
> "Dandelions are ignored or attacked, never nurtured or cared for, and yet they always bloom profusely. They demand no pampering or special attention to yield their bright blossoms; they pop up in fields, in lawns, and between cracks in the sidewalk, even in the best neighborhoods. Can you imagine trying to grow them in a garden? They'd sneak through the boundaries and pop their sunny yellow faces up in the surrounding lawn. They would never stay put!
>
> "Christians should be more like dandelions. Our sunny yellow faces should be a reminder that simple faith has deep roots that are impossible to dislodge. Our vast number would show the world that even though we are not fancy or pampered we are evident everywhere, even in the best neighborhoods.

> "We should be as easily accessible as a dandelion. Jesus was. We need to get out of our gardens and jump across the boundaries that keep us where people expect to find us. We need to show our sunny yellow faces in all the spots that need a little brightening up–the crack in the sidewalk or the lawn of a country club."

My thoughts. "Trees in a hurricane can be completely uprooted, and they die. How will the "hurricanes" of life find me? Shallow rooted in Jesus – or deep?"

An observation: Some flowers (ex. petunias) wilt when water is put directly on their blossoms. Do I wilt under the "rain" of circumstances?

From my journal. "I had the opportunity to visit the Biltmore gardens. As I neared one part, a wonderful fragrance preceded finding wild azaleas. I wondered, "What fragrance comes from my garden? Does it go before me? Does it introduce others to the beauty of my garden? Has the "burial" of my flesh been "prepared" with the fragrance of the Holy Spirit? What spices have been used: circumstances, trials, events, my past sins now forgiven?

"Many times when I hug someone, the fragrance they are wearing is left behind on my clothing or skin. Do I leave behind a sweet smell? My mother's favorite perfume was Estee Lauder Youth Dew. I never smell it now without remembering my mother. What is my identifying fragrance?"

How does what is planted in my garden make the Lord look? A seed can only be what it's programmed to be. Botanists "play around" with seeds and pollens to create mutations and hybrids and do genetic engineering. Are we allowing Satan to "fiddle" with our lives? Or are we striving to be how God "programmed" us to be? Are we real or phony? Ephesians 5:1 to 6:18. Imitate Christ like children do their parents: in acts, words, nature, ways, grace, spirit, and attitude.

At least once a week (during the growing season) I walk in my gardens at home. I look at all the new buds and those which have recently opened. They're beautiful. I look for new growth on plants recently planted. I prune the dead heads when the blossoms have faded. I harvest seeds which I can plant next season. I look for disease and insects, and treat them to stop their spread. I water the hanging plants, and others which may need a little extra moisture, because they've begun to droop from the heat. I look into Mrs. Wren's nest to see how the babies are doing. Soon she, or Mr. Wren are scolding me for peeking.

The first roses of summer are beautiful. But unless they are properly fed, watered, pruned, and treated for disease, they will become sickly: leaves will lose their shine, buds will fail to form or will not open, and the plant will lose its beauty. Unless the blossoms are taken off, when finished, the plant will develop hips, go dormant, and have no more beauty this season.

Even during dormant times I walk around the gardens, thinking about how a particular plant performed during its recent season. I plan to move it, if necessary, to put it in a better place where it may be better able to reach it's potential. I also prune off dead or diseased growth.

When the Lord walks in my spiritual garden He looks for growth, beauty, disease, and He prunes and waters me with His word. He uses all kinds of circumstances to accomplish this husbandry. He loves the garden which I am. He wants me to be beautiful and productive.

So how is your garden growing?

BIBLICAL HERBS

"God Almighty first planted a garden, and, indeed it

is the purest of human pleasure." Frances Bacon

Herbs have been an important part of the earth since the beginning. Their uses range from medicinal, culinary, cosmetic, and disinfectant, and they have monetary value. Listed below are references to their different uses in history, as found in the Bible.

Aloe (aloe vera)
Numbers 24:6. "Like valleys they spread out like gardens beside a river, like aloe planted by the Lord, like cedars beside the waters." Translated, the name means patience. Some religions planted aloe at the foot of a grave to test the corpse's "patience" between burial and resurrection. Aloe is now known to have been one of Cleopatra's beauty secrets.

Coriander (coriandrum sativum)
Exodus 16:31. "The people of Israel called the bread Manna." It was white like coriander seed and tasted like wafers made with honey.

Costmary (Chrysanthemum balsamita)
Costmary was said to relieve Mary's pain during Jesus' birth. It was called "Bible leaf." The puritans used it as a fragrant bookmark and to relieve their hunger during the long sermons.

Garlic (allium sativum)
Numbers 11:5. "We remember the fish we ate in Egypt at no cost - also the cucumbers, melons, leeks, onions, and garlic." Garlic was highly esteemed by the Egyptians who gave the slaves who were building the great pyramid a daily supply for strength. Romans believed in garlic's strengthening process and fed it to their soldiers before battle. It has been used for centuries to ward off evil, and in

modern myth it serves as protection from vampires.

Hyssop (labiate)

Psalm 51:7. "Purge me with hyssop, and I shall be clean." It was used to purify the temples and to cleanse the lepers. Research has discovered that the mold that produces penicillin grows on its leaf. This could have acted as an antibiotic protection when lepers were bathed in hyssop.

Lady's bedstraw (galum verum)

Legend says it was used for the Christ child's manger bed.

Rose (rosa)

Song of Solomon 2:1. "I am the rose of Sharon. The lily of the valley." The word rose comes from the Greek word meaning "red." It is called "the gift of the angels." The rose reigns supreme in its beauty and fragrance. Rose hips were used as a source of vitamin C during World War II when oranges and vegetables were unobtainable.

Rosemary (rosemary officinalis)

Rosemary was considered a sacred ceremonial herb symbolizing remembrance at funerals, and fidelity at weddings. One legend says that it will never grow higher than Christ, and having outlived the thirty-three years of our Lord's life, will grow only outward rather than upward.

Rue (ruta graveolens)

Luke 11:42. "But woe unto you, Pharisees, for you tithe mint and rue and all manner of herbs." Rue's common name is "herb of grace." Sprigs of it were used to sprinkle holy water before high mass. According to scripture, it held a place of value to be used as a tithe.

Wormwood (artemisia absinthium)

Jeremiah 23:15. "Behold, I am going to feed them wormwood and make them drink poisonous water." Wormwood is one of the most bitter herbs. Absinthe has been banned from most countries due to the alarming effect of this habit-forming drink, including hallucinations and epileptic-like seizures. Habitual use leads to irreparable damage to the nervous system, general paralysis and death.

Notes

By permission of John L. Hart FLP, and Creators Syndicate, Inc.

CHAPTER THREE

COMPANION PLANTING

Source: *Encyclopedia of Organic Gardening*, J. I. Rodale and Staff

Wherever plants grow without cultivation there is a colorful mixture of plants, which, in accordance with the soil type and local climatic conditions, are able to live together and mutually complement each other. Such a mixed culture of plants in nature is called a "natural plant association." The plants in an association are such that they utilize to the fullest extent such environmental factors as light, moisture, and soil. Plants that require less light live in the shade of those which must have full light. Also the roots of some plants live close to the surface, while those of others penetrate to greater depths.

The plants in an association do not all grow and fruit at the same time in the growing season. Some plants hurry into growth and flowering early in the season, before those which might cut off their source of light produce leaves at all. The different kinds of plants in an association produce an endless succession of green leaves, flowers, and fruits from early spring to killing autumn frosts.

In planting our vegetable garden, we may well imitate, so far as possible, nature's mixed plantings, using such plants as are mutually compatible and make demands on the environment at different times.

Some plants, which have a beneficial effect upon the garden by virtue of the peculiar character of their growth, their scent, and their root formation and soil demands, have a beneficial effect upon the garden. Odoriferous plants, including those with aromatic oils, play an important part in determining just which insects visit the garden.

It is not a matter of indifference in what associations plants are grown. Good plant neighbors are those whose roots occupy different levels in the soil or find in each other's company the light requirements which best suit them. Pole beans planted with sunflowers grow most unsatisfactorily as a result of root and light interference. Sunflowers and potatoes are equally incompatible, and we run the risk of getting stunted vines and small potatoes. Other incompatible combinations are tomatoes and fennel, tomatoes and kohlrabi, pole beans and beets, pole beans and kohlrabi, and red and black raspberries.

Compatible combinations of vegetables are cabbage and beans, beets and onions, celeriac and leeks, cucumbers and sweet corn, leeks and beans, carrots and peas, cucumbers and beans, kohlrabi and beets, onions and beets, early potatoes and horse radish, tomatoes and parsley, bush beans and celery, and cucumbers and bush beans.

Compatible plants are those which supplement each other in the soil as well as above the ground. The compatibility of celery and leek, for instance, consists in the upright nature of the leek thus finding room near the bushy celery plant, and both are potash-lovers. Lettuce and kohlrabi, for instance, are compatible for intercropping, as the lettuce will be harvested by the time the larger kohlrabi plants need all the space in the row. Mixed cultures, as in intercropping, provide a more complete ground cover, thus preventing the ground from crusting and drying out, and holds the weeds in check.

Some important likes and dislikes of plants mentioned in the book *Biodynamic Farming and*

Gardening by Dr. Ehrenfried Pfeiffer:

Asparagus. The asparagus beetle is repelled by tomatoes growing close to the asparagus plants.

Cabbage. To repel the cabbage maggot, plant mint, hemp, tomatoes, rosemary or sage in the next row.

Carrots. Peas are good for them when growing nearby.

Celery. Plant bush beans in the next row.

Cucumber. Plant beans or corn next to them. Also peas and bush beans.

Herbs. Aromatic herbs as border plants are helpful.

Onions. Do well with beans. In poor soil, camomile sown thinly between will help.

Potatoes. Corn is a natural and beneficial neighbor. Early potatoes like beans to grow nearby.

Radish. Will do extra well and become tender if there is a row of lettuce growing on each side of them.

Tomatoes. Plant parsley in the next bed.

Turnips. Peas are excellent neighbors.

Negative effects.

Fennel. Do not plant them near tomatoes or bush beans.

Tomatoes. Do not plant next to kohlrabi.

<u>FOR COLOR.</u> Interplant perennials with bulbs to get more color without adding maintenance chores. Bulbs, like crocuses, daffodils, and tulips make great companions for perennial flowers because they willingly share the same space. The bulbs lie low and emerge early, so they won't disrupt your perennials' performance, and they make good

location markers for slow-to-show perennials. If you plant hostas over your bulb bed, when the bulb foliage dies, the hosta leaves cover the dying leaves. (Note: daffodil leaves should never be cut off before they are completely dead. Otherwise energy for next year's blooming may be hindered. And "braiding" them is not a good idea for the same reason.)

FOR DISEASE CONTROL. For areas where verticillium wilt (a fungal disease) is a problem, plant marigolds in April, then turn them under with a tiller or shovel in June. (A chemical in the marigold foliage gets rid of the fungus in the soil.) That way you can plant more marigolds with a later crop, like tomatoes and you won't lose a season's harvest of color.

FOR PEST CONTROL. Plant herbs to keep cabbage butterflies and their voracious offspring, called imported cabbageworms, out of your cabbage patch. Grow a bed full of catmint and hyssop near cabbage. The butterflies are either distracted by it or attracted to it and won't eat the cabbage.

Radishes can protect your squash from squash borers. Plant radish seeds in a 1-foot diameter circle and plant the squash in the center of the circle. Keep enough there so that their leaves can touch.

UNDER TREES. Pick perennials that like the same conditions that the trees do. Use water-hungry perennials around trees which like moist soil and drought-tolerant plants around trees which like drier conditions. (Note: Take special note of how much sun/shade the tree allows for whatever may grow beneath it.)

FOR WEED CONTROL. Clover keeps corn weed-free (besides providing extra nitrogen for the soil). Give the corn a month's head start and then sow any kind of clover.

Oats crowd out early spring weeds and improve

the soil when they break down into organic matter around garlic.

Lettuce, chard, or spinach make a good mulch under pole bean trellises. The lettuce leaves form a canopy that shades out weeds.

Marigolds are a great plant to put all around your vegetable garden. Besides adding such great "hot" color, their smell keeps out some critters and insects.

SPIRITUAL APPLICATION

My God sticks closer than a brother. He will never leave me or forsake me.

Who are the companions of your life? They can have an impact on what kind of soil is in your heart's garden and what kind of "plants" are growing there.

In 1997, I clipped a newspaper article from the Associated Press entitled, "Researchers: Well-rounded people get fewer colds." In summary, it said "people with few social outlets were four times as likely to get sick as people busy with six or more activities," and "with each added relationship you have, the less likely you are to become ill." The article "ruled out the possibility that they had developed immunity to colds from their exposure to many kinds of germs from different people."

The Bible has much to say about companions, calling them fellow workers, prisoners, laborers, soldiers, heirs, servants, helpers, citizens, to name a few. They can be your personal friend, associate, comrade, mate, partner, guide, or mentor.

2 Corinthians 6:14-18 NIV gives guidance about being unequally yoked, and that applies to more than in marriage. "Do not be yoked together with unbelievers. For what do righteousness and wickedness have in common? Or what fellowship can light have with darkness? What harmony is there between Christ and Belial? What does a believer have in common with an unbeliever? What agreement is there between the temple of God and idols? For we are the temple of the living God. As God has said: 'I will live with them and walk among them, and I will be their God, and they will be My people.' Therefore come out from them and be separate." And verse 1 of chapter 7, "Since we have these promises, dear friends, let us purify ourselves

from everything that contaminates body and spirit, perfecting holiness out of reverence for God."

In *Growing Strong in the Seasons of Life,* Multnomah Press, Charles Swindoll writes, "A Sheltering Tree."

> "Shortly before his death, Samuel Taylor Coleridge wrote *Youth and Age* in which he reflected over his past and the strength of his earlier years. He wrote, for example: 'Nought cared this body for wind or weather, When youth and I lived in it together'...But, to me, the most moving line in this quaint work is the statement. 'Friendship is a sheltering tree.'
>
> "How true...how terribly true! When the searing rays of adversity's sun burn their way into our day, there's nothing quite like a sheltering tree–a true friend–to give us relief in its cool shade. Its massive trunk of understanding gives security as its thick leaves of love wash our face and wipe our brow. Beneath its branches has rested many a discouraged soul.
>
> "Let me name a few. Elijah was ready to quit. Depressed and threatened, he turned in his prophet's badge and wrote out his resignation. God refused to accept either. He gave him rest, good food, and a tree named Elisha–who, according to Elijah's own testimony, 'ministered to him' (1 Kings 19:19-21). In the analogy of Coleridge, Elijah rested in the shade of Elisha's 'sheltering

tree.'

"Paul had a similar experience. In fact, the trees in his life significantly sustained him. There was a Barnabas who stood by him when everyone else ran from him (Acts 9:26-27); (11:25-26). There was Silas, his traveling companion over many an otherwise lonely mile (Acts 15:40-41). When you add Dr. Luke and Timothy and Onesiphorus and Epaphroditus and Aquila and Priscilla, you find a veritable *forest* of sheltering trees in that great man's life. Even Jesus enjoyed Lazarus, Martha, and Mary. Even *He* was refreshed beneath those sheltering branches from Bethany (John 11:5).

"But of all of the trees that God placed beside His choice servants, one human redwood looms the largest, in my opinion. David was hunted and haunted by madman, Saul. The king's single objective was to witness with his own eyes David's corpse. Between Saul and David, however, stood a sheltering tree named Jonathan, who neither shook nor shed in that precarious place. No matter how hard he tried, Saul could not chop down that tree! Loyal and dependable, Jonathan assured David, 'Whatever you say, I will do for you.' (1 Samuel 20:4). No limits. No conditions. No bargains. No reservations. Best of all, when things were at their worst, he 'went to David...and encouraged him in God.' (1 Samuel 23:16). Why? Why would he provide such a refreshment? Because he was committed to the basic principles of a friendship. Because 'he loved him as he loved himself' (1 Samuel 18:1). It was love that knit their hearts together. The kind of love that causes men to lay down their lives for their friends, as Jesus put it (John 15:13). No greater love exists on this globe.

"Beneath whose branches are *you* refreshed, dear reader? Or, dare I ask, who rests beneath *yours*? Occasionally, I run across an independent soul who shuns the idea that he needs such shelter, feeling that trees are for the immature, the spiritual babes, or those who haven't learned to trust only in the Lord. It is *that* person I most pity, for his horizontal contacts are invariably superficial and shallow. Worst of all, his closing years on earth will be spent in the loneliest spot imaginable–a hot, treeless desert.

"So then, let's be busy about the business of watering and pruning and cultivating our trees, shall we? Would I be more accurate if I added *planting* a few? Growing them takes time, you know...and you may really need a few when the heat rises and the winds begin to blow.

"But I should remind you that a real, genuine, deep, solid friend is exceedingly rare. Either you're still looking through the forest...or, like me (thank God), you're enjoying shade and shelter today beside your God-given tree."

Psalm 119:63 CEV "I choose as my friends everyone who worships you and follows your teachings."

Proverbs 13:20 CEV "Wise friends make you wise, but you hurt yourself by going around with fools."

Proverbs 28:7 CEV "It makes good sense to obey the Law of God, but you disgrace your parents if you make friends with worthless nobodies."

An old saying: "Lay down with dogs, and you get up with fleas!"

The Holy Spirit is described as the paraclete–an advocate or intercessor, summoned to aid. Comforter, helper, Spirit of Truth. When Jesus went back to Heaven, He sent the Holy Spirit to us, a person like Himself. (John 14:15-17).

My Contemporary English Bible (CEV), Thomas Nelson Publishers, has a short teaching, "How can I tell if a friendship is unhealthy?" Paul sets certain limits (2 Corinthians 6:14-18) on our relationships with unbelievers. Paul doesn't name specific issues such as marriage; the Bible addresses that concern elsewhere. He does say that, as a general rule, you must decide whether certain alliances and experiences with unbelievers will weaken your commitment to Christ.

> "In Corinth, idol worship was a fundamental part of life. Since Christ lived in the Corinthian believers, they had to make a complete break with their culture. Paul's language is strong because the stakes are high (5:15). Do certain friendships, relatives, or jobs cause you to dishonor God or compromise your commitment to him? Prayerfully consider who and what you're involved in. Ask advice from wise, believing friends for perspective and support. God

promises to bless you for honoring him above all others. His promise is that blessings come in this life–and the next."

Proverbs 27:17 "Just as iron sharpens iron, friends sharpen the minds of each other." And verse 19, "You see your face in a mirror and your thoughts in the minds of others."

A "test" for relationships is to place the name of your friend in place of "love" in 1 Corinthians 13:4-8. What's the score?

Ecclesiastes 4:12, "Any enemy might defeat one person, but two people together can defend themselves."

Proverbs 17:17, "A friend loves at all times, and a brother is born for adversity."

Proverbs 18:24, "A man of many companions may come to ruin, but there is a friend who sticks closer than a brother."

Proverbs 27:6, "Wounds from a friend can be trusted, but an enemy multiplies kisses."

In Matthew 13:24-25, Jesus talks about weed seeds being sown among good seeds. The gospel and true believers will be planted throughout the world, and Satan will also plant his followers among them to counteract God's 'truth,' undermining the authority of the Word. Verse 30 indicates both will grow together. Believers must be alert to these. Know the Word. Watch for false teachers; discern character, motives, test fruit, are they teaching the inspiration and authority of scripture?

An article in the newspaper from Gannett News Service is titled, "Study. Hugging warms the heart, and also may protect it."

It reads: "Cuddling may be good medicine for the heart. A brief hug and 10 minutes of hand holding with a romantic partner greatly reduces the harmful physical effect of stress, according to a recent American Psychosomatic Society meeting.

> "Loving contact before a tough day at work could carry over and protect you throughout the day."

The article tells how the study was done and reported that blood pressure soared in the no-contact people. Heart rate increased 10 beats a minute for huggers. It continued, suggesting that humans are "hard-wired" to thrive as social animals. Research also showed that touch lowers the output of cortisol, a stress hormone. When cortisol dips, there's a surge of two "feel good" brain chemicals, serotonin and dopamine.

It states that some studies have indicated that touch among friends might be helpful but doesn't produce nearly as much physical stress relief as contact with a partner, and suggests this may be one reason isolated, lonely people tend to have poorer health. One researcher stated that although ours is a youth-oriented culture, older adults may benefit most from touch, and concludes by writing, "The older you are, the more fragile you are physically, so contact becomes increasingly important for good health."

<u>Daily Survival.</u> (sent to me by email)
Items needed: Mint, candy kiss, tea bag, eraser, rubber band, toothpick, chewing gum, band aid, and pencil. Why?????

<u>Toothpick.</u> To remind you to pick out the good qualities in others. Matthew 7:1.

<u>Rubber band.</u> To remind you to be flexible. Things might not always go the way you want, but they will work out. Romans 8:28.

<u>Band aid.</u> To remind you to heal hurt feelings; yours or someone else's. Colossians 3:12-14.

<u>Pencil</u>. To remind you to list your blessings every day. Ephesians 1:3.

<u>Eraser.</u> To remind you that everyone makes mistakes, and it's okay. Genesis 50:15-21.

<u>Chewing gum.</u> To remind you to stick to it, and you can accomplish anything. Philippians 4:13.

<u>Mint.</u> To remind you that you are worth a lot. John 3:16-17.

<u>Candy kiss.</u> To remind you that everyone needs a kiss or a hug every day. John 4:7.

<u>Tea bag.</u> To remind you to relax daily and look over your list of blessings. 1 Thessalonians 5:18.

<u>Friendship's smile.</u>

"Lord, thank You for loyal, loving friends
Who are there in winter or springtime faithfully.
New acquaintances are easy to come by,
But true friendship is extremely rare.
A friend always sees the best in you,
Although they've known you at your worst.
They laugh with you in the good times,
When storms threaten, they'll be there first.
They'll offer a shoulder to rest your head on
When tears are welling in your eyes,
Take a walk down friendship's path with you
And help chase away those stormy skies.
Lord, thank You for all the gifts You give me.
Each one makes our life seem more worthwhile.
But one of the finest gifts you've given us
Is the warmth of friendship's loving smile.
- Anonymous

Notes

CHAPTER FOUR

FERTILIZERS/NOURISHMENT

Source: *The Tennessee Master Gardner Handbook*, University of Tennessee Agricultural Extension Service.

Nourish: To furnish food or other material to sustain the life and promote the growth of a living plant.

In addition to light, air, water, and space for roots, growing plants need a supply of nutrients – elements necessary to carry out their life processes.

If you have had your soil tested, the test has indicated if nutrients are missing, and the rate at which they should be applied to make your soil healthier in order to give you more beautiful and plentiful flowers, or a more prolific vegetable garden or productive orchard.

Because our East Tennessee soil is quite acid, its pH may need to be raised. The primary function of lime is to correct the acid soil. Pelletized lime is much easier to spread and creates less dust when it is added to your lawn or garden. The best time for spreading it is in the fall because the soil is drier. It should not be applied every year. Follow the distribution amounts listed on the container.

When purchasing fertilizer for your yard or garden, the bag will have three numbers, referring to how much of an element there is in the material, based on the percentage of weight of nitrogen (N), phosphorus (P), and potassium (K). For example, if you have a 100 pound bag of 10-10-10, there are 10 pounds of N, 10 pounds of P, and 10 pounds of K. The other 70 pounds is filler. The filler helps to evenly spread the fertilizer and avoids burning plants with too much fertilizer. Some common fillers are clay, vermiculite, fuller's earth and diatomaceous earth.

Nitrogen is necessary for the greening of plants; their most important element. It comes only from other sources, primarily from decomposing organic material. Rainfall carries it to the soil. Large amounts are needed for the plant to live and reproduce. It is easily lost by irrigation and rainfall leaching. (It can be lost from the soil, and thus not be available to the plants if wood chips are introduced into the soil, by tilling in. This, however, will only be for a season, for the wood product will break down and then enrich the soil.) This is the first number shown on a container of fertilizer you buy. Example: 21-10-10 indicates 21% of the product is nitrogen.

Phosphorus is necessary for the production of flowers and fruits. It does not dissolve and move through the soil. As roots contact the soil, they absorb the phosphorus that is in the soil. The soil particles have to release it as the roots move into fresh areas. Therefore, the gardener needs to dig down to where the roots are when applying phosphorus. It is the second number of the three listed on the container. Example: 10-21-10 would let you know this product will enhance the blooming or fruiting (whatever reason you're applying it) of your plant or tree.

Potassium is necessary for healthy roots. It exists naturally in the soil from minerals, fertilizers or crop residues. It also needs to be near the roots. (Rotten bananas, or just the peels, are a good source of potassium. Put them in your blender with a little water, scratch the surface of the soil around your plant (roses love it!) and pour it on. (My staghorn fern almost raises its fronds in delight when I put some inside its cowl!) It's the third number on the package.

Other necessary nutrients, needed in smaller amounts, for healthy plants, are calcium (for cell growth), magnesium (for leaves), sulfur (essential for plant cells), iron (for chlorophyll formation), zinc and manganese (triggers utilization of nutrients). The last three, found in chelated form, are a form to be used by the roots.

A complete fertilizer contains N, P and K. An incomplete fertilizer will be missing one or more of these major components. (An example of incomplete may have a label listing 34-0-0, which indicates it's 34% nitrogen and 66% filler. That's what you'd use to get a quick green fix for your lawn!)

Special purpose fertilizers are packaged for certain uses or types of plants, such as camellia food, rhododendron and azalea food or rose food.

Slow-release fertilizers are designed to release nutrients at the same rate they are taken up by the plants. They contain one or more essential nutrients which are released or made available to the plant over an extended time through, 1) materials that dissolve slowly, 2) materials from which the nitrogen is released by the action of microorganisms, and 3) granular materials with membranes made of resin or sulfur that control the rate of nutrient released from the granules into the soil. Slow-release fertilizers need not be applied as frequently as other fertilizers and higher amounts can be applied without as much danger of burn.

Organic fertilizers have nutrients contained in the product derived solely from the remains of a once-living organism. Cottonseed meal, blood meal, bone meal, hoof and horn meal, and all manures are examples of organic fertilizers. Organic fertilizers are relatively low in concentrations of actual nutrients, but may perform other soil-conditioning functions, including increasing the organic matter content of the soil, improving soil physical properties and increasing microorganism activity.

Organic fertilizers can be made of common

household products. Jerry Baker, who calls himself "America's Master Gardener," has many publications which have recipes using ordinary household products, like peroxide, alcohol, dish soap, tea, coffee, etc.

Systemics are fertilizers mixed with insecticides to kill harmful bugs by going through the roots and into the system of the plant. The bugs are killed as they eat the plant, or suck its juices. (Systemics are often used on roses to fight aphids.)

Homemade fertilizers!

Before preparing your flower beds, stop by a "coffee shop" and ask for the coffee grounds they throw away. These can be used in compost piles or worm bins, or to add nitrogen to the soil.

Kitchen waste tea. (This can get really stinky, so put it in a large container with a tight fitting lid and keep it away from the house while it's "cooking.")
Fish parts (when cleaning fish, it's the innards, fins, skin, heads, etc.)
Ground banana peels (whole bananas, ground, can be used too)
Coffee grounds
Tea leaves
Egg shells, dried and crushed
Soak it all in three times as much water as it amounts to when mixed together. Cover it for a month and let it "cook." Strain it, dilute it until it looks like weak tea, and use it on outdoor plants. If it is too strong it can burn the roots of your plants.

Compost tea.
Fill a large bucket or 8-gallon tub with water.

Pour 2 pounds of compost into a burlap bag and tie the top closed. Put the bag in the tub and drape it over the side to steep in the water.
When the mixture is the color of strong coffee (this takes about 10 days), fill a watering can or bucket halfway with it, then dilute it by adding water until it is the color of weak tea. Leave the bag in the tub, adding water as the level drops. You can refill the tub twice before replacing the compost.

Feed container plants and other outdoor plants once a month with this "food."

<u>Manure tea.</u>
Make it the same way as compost tea, substituting manure for the compost.

SPIRITUAL APPLICATION

God is my nourishment. Philippians 4:13 He tells me I can do everything through Him Who strengthens me.

September 12, *The Heart of the Home*, a devotional. "God created us with an overwhelming desire to soar. Our desire to develop and use every ounce of potential He's placed in us is not egotistical. He designed us to be tremendously productive and 'to mount up with wings like eagles,' realistically, dreaming of what He can do with our potential." Carl Kent, *Secret Passions of the Christian Woman.*

I have ferns hanging on the front porch. I was able to keep them all through the winter; I am so proud of myself that they didn't die. (My sweet husband faithfully brought them into the workshop every night it was supposed to freeze, and then rehung them on the porch when the weather was to be warmer.) In the spring I started putting a little Miracle Gro in their water and now they need to be repotted, they have grown so much.

This "miracle grow" (the Bible) watered into your life frequently, can make you spiritually healthier, with beauty that blesses others. Your "roots" will increase. Add it to your life every day. Don't let your busyness keep you from getting nourished.

Our text says nitrogen is the most important food a plant needs. That represents the Father, the Architect of our lives. Potassium, to nourish our roots, is the Son, the Builder of our lives. The Holy Spirit, our Beautifier, is represented by phosphorus, because He puts the fruits of the Spirit in our lives.

The text defines "nourish," as furnishing food or other material to sustain the life and promote the growth of a living plant; to feed or support, to bring up or train, educate.

The garden of our lives needs nourishment and nurturing. Just as a garden at our home needs three major nutrients, and many lesser ones, so we need to feed and provide spiritual food for ourselves.

The more important is a relationship with the Father, through Jesus, and our lives beautified by the Holy Spirit.

Colossians 2:7, "Keep your roots deep in Him. Build your lives on Him. Become stronger in your faith."

1 Timothy 4:6, " – you will be a good servant of Christ Jesus as you feed yourself spiritually on the words of faith and of the true teaching which you have followed."

Ephesians 5:29, "No one ever hates his own body. Instead he feeds it and takes care of it, just as Christ does the church."

Colossians 2:19, "Under Christ's control the whole body is nourished and held together by its joints and ligaments and it grows as God wants it to grow."

Acts 3:19, 20, "After repenting – times of refreshing will come from the presence of the Lord."

As in our text, there are three major nutrients; there are many others which will enhance us spiritually:

<u>Prayer</u>.

1 Timothy 2:8, "I want men everywhere to lift up holy hands in prayer."

1 Thessolonians 5:17, "Pray continually (without ceasing)."

A newspaper article a few years ago stated, "Medical workers are being urged by some prominent doctors to suggest their patients take two prayers–along with their medication–and call them in the morning. Physicians specializing in heart disease, psychiatry, pediatrics, and other areas told colleagues at a 'Spirituality in Health Care' conference that slowing down, praying, meditating and being loved–along with traditional medications and surgeries–can heal.

"Rabbits who were stroked, loved, and nurtured had 60% less plaque in their arteries.

"It's about undoing and letting go. It's not something that you chose to make you happy. It's something you already have. It's a quieting of the mind."

Hayford's Bible Handbook, Thomas Nelson Publishers, states, "The night before His crucifixion, Jesus underscored the privileged pathway of prayer now being opened to His own through His cross (John 16:24). 'Until now you have asked nothing in My name. Ask, and you will receive, that your joy may be full.' By His own emphasis, Jesus placed prayer at the heart of Christian living. When the pulse is steady and the body exercised in this practice, every other facet of life flows with health, as the individual is fed by God's Word."

Spending time in the Word. Join a Bible study group.

Psalm 119:11, "I have hidden Your word in my heart that I might not sin against You."

Psalm 119:24, "Your statutes are my delight, they are my counselors."

Psalm 119:45, "I will walk about in freedom, for I have sought out Your precepts."

Psalm 119:92, "If Your law had not been my delight, I would have perished in my affliction."

Psalm 119:98, "Your commands make me wiser than my enemies, for (Your commands) are ever with me."

Psalm 119:103, "How sweet are Your words to my taste, sweeter than honey in my mouth!"

Psalm 119:105, "Your word is a lamp to my feet and a light for my path."

Psalm 119:111, "Your statutes are my heritage forever; they are the joy of my heart."

Psalm 119:152, "Long ago I learned from Your statutes that You established them to last forever."

Psalm 119:165, "Great peace have they who love Your law, and nothing can make them stumble."

Get together with other Christians. Hebrews 10:25 NIV, "Let us not give up meeting together, as some are in the habit of doing, but let us encourage one another."

Giving. Luke 6:38 GNB, "Give to others and God will give to you. Indeed, you will receive a full measure, a generous helping, poured into your hands–all that you can hold. The measure you use for others is the one that God will use for you."

Resting. Psalm 23:2, "He makes me to lie down." Commentary from *Full Life Study Bible*, "Because of the presence and nearness of the Shepherd, I can lie down in peace, free from all fear. The Holy Spirit, as my Comforter, Counselor, and Helper, communicates Christ's shepherdly care and presence to me. My confident rest in His presence will be experienced in green pastures, in Jesus and the Word of God, which are necessary for an abundant life. He leads me beside quiet waters of His Holy Spirit."

Matthew 11:28, "Come to Me all you who are weak and heavy laden, and I will give you rest. My yoke is easy and My burden is light. I am gentle and humble in spirit, and you will find rest."

Hebrews 4:9-10, "There remains then, a Sabbath rest for the people of God; for anyone who enters God's rest also rests from his own work, just as God did from His." (Genesis 2:2)

Exodus 23:10-11, "Let your land rest in the 7th year."

I have a friend, Martha, who went for two years to American Samoa with her husband who was working for the American government as an accountant. While they were there, she busied herself with a vacation Bible school for the Samoan children. She had to travel out into the primitive bush country and undergo many cultural challenges which were distasteful to her: lizards running around at night on the netting that covered their bed, droppings falling on them, rats, eating food (like fish with the heads still on and the eyes staring at her!) prepared by the tribal chiefs whom she visited in order to get permission to teach their children. The hardships were so severe, although Martha learned to love the Samoan people, that they came home before their time was over. They had to leave everything they owned behind because the American government would not move back their belongings unless they completed their time.

Martha and her husband are very dedicated Christians. Yet, when they returned, the Lord did not open any areas of ministry to them in the Oregon area for many years. Martha was quite puzzled about this until, as we talked, we realized the Lord was letting them rest. The last contact I had with them, they were again active in ministry.

<u>Other ways to nourish yourself</u>.
Soak in a tub of hot bubbles or bath oil.
Read a book.
Have lunch with a friend.
Have a night out with some significant person.
Get a new hairdo.
Get counseling, if you need it. (Sometimes, just talking to a trusted friend helps you sort through what may be bothering you.)
Dealing with depression, Proverbs 17:22, "A cheerful heart is good medicine, but a crushed spirit dries up the bones."

Health magazine ran an article in 1997 stating, "Severe depression may be bone-wearing in more than just a figurative sense. Researchers have found that the bones of 40-something women who suffer from depression are far weaker than those of women who don't. Researchers measured the bone density of 24 women who had suffered at least one three-month episode of depression. They compared the measurements with those of a group of women who had never been depressed, but were comparable in age, weight, menopausal status, and race. The depressed women's bones were 6.5% less dense at the spine and 10-15% less dense at the hip. That level of bone loss can raise a woman's risk of hip fracture by 40% over a ten-year period."

Isaiah 61:3, "---for grieving, not ashes, but beauty
---for mourning, the oil of gladness,
---for heaviness and despair (depression), a garment of praise."

Buy yourself something, "just because."
Eat healthier. (Daniel 1:12-16)
Exercise regularly. (1 Timothy 4:8)

Rich Buhler, *New Choices, New Boundaries,* writes, "God has constructed human beings with a natural need to be nourished. Yet the word "nourishment" has almost no practical meaning for us. It has been years since we made even a tiny choice that could be called nourishing. If we lack nourishment, we will know it by the ache and the longing in our bodies, our hearts and our spirits.

> "What motivates the actions we take to satisfy our inner hunger–which still leaves us starving: the approval of others, obligations.
>
> "What can I do to nourish me?
> 1. Commit my life to Christ.
> 2. Spend time with those from whom I can receive, not give.
> 3. Give gifts to myself.
> 4. Take the responsibility for my own nourishment; don't assume others

know what I want or need.

5. Allow solitude.

"Needed nourishment sources: family, friends, jobs, schools, fellowship, God's word, hobbies, enjoying the world around you. Note: some sources can lead to addiction: food, drugs, alcohol, sex, shopping, exercising.

"Failure can nourish us. Devastation can nourish richly. Not everything that is nourishing tastes good and not everything that tastes good is nourishing. (1 Thessalonians 5:18, Romans 8:28).

"Nourishment begins with you; you are responsible to nourish yourself. It should come from more than one source. Get involved with nourishing activities. Enrich your spiritual life. Give yourself to others. Accomplish goals. Spend time alone."

Obstacles to properly nourishing yourself may include guilt, fear, and perfectionism. You may think you do not deserve to "pamper" yourself. You may fear what others may think. Perfectionism may cause you to not be able to let go of a project when it is finished, thereby continuing on infinitum to exhaustion. These may be tools of the enemy to keep you from being refreshed so that you will be more effective in ministry in whatever form it takes.

In the Bible, Jesus is described as nourishing His bride–the Church–and caring for her tenderly (Ephesians 5:29 and following), as a gardener cares for a precious plant. When a gardener notices that a plant is fading and withering, the gardener won't beat it with a hoe and give it lectures about how faded it looks. Efforts will be renewed to care for the plant so it will regain its strength and grow.

Fruits of the Spirit come from 'trees' whose roots are in good soil. These trees are nourished through those roots from that soil. When the roots are withered because of improper care and nourishment, they are unable to supply the branches with the nutrition that causes fruit to form. If fruit does form, it is small and sour.

When a tree has luscious fruit, you know all conditions have been properly met.

The fruits of a Christian's life are like that. Are they abundant? Are they able to minister life and health? Are they attractive to look at?

We bought some peaches which looked so beautiful. Their outward appearance made my mouth water. We anticipated a taste treat. But when we bit into those peaches, they were dry and mealy.

A person may 'look' and 'act' like a wonderful Christian. He or she may say all the right things, but what happens when they are put to the test and their 'fruit' is tasted?

The peaches we bought had been picked from the tree while they were still green. They were not fully mature. Their maturing came from sitting in boxes waiting to be marketed. They had been separated from their source before they ripened "in due season." They didn't get to finish receiving whatever made them delicious to the tongue.

Many Christians become separated from the Word, prayer, and fellowship. Their 'fruit' is tasteless–not able to produce that which nourishes another.

What is your source? Are you still connected to Jesus? Will you be able to minister spiritual life and health to someone else? Do you know how to nourish yourself?

Or will you be rejected and discarded?

WORDS OF WISDOM

Laughter appears to have a healthy effect on every organ. The involvement of the lungs and diaphragm causes increased uptake of oxygen, which nourishes every part of the body.

In a "Dear Abby" column I read, " I don't blame you for being angry. But please don't make it a career. Hate corrodes the vessel that carries it."

A newspaper article: "The link between faith and healing is getting a closer look from more and more doctors. A survey of the American Academy of Family Physicians found 99% of doctors believe there is an important relationship between the spirit and flesh.

From *USA Weekend*, October 10-12, 2003. "Diabetes: Laughter lowers blood sugar. Laughing can lower blood sugar. A Japanese study reported in *Diabetes Care* found blood sugar levels were lower in people who laughed after a meal than in people who didn't laugh. Why? Researchers don't know yet, but they say daily laughter can help control diabetics' blood sugar. —Peggy J. Noonan

Tips for creating a simple life. Gannett News Service.

> "**Understand yourself.** Look inside to find what makes you happy.
>
> "**Cooperate.** Get together with friends to make things easier and economical: potlucks, shared child care, car pooling.
>
> "**Go slowly.** Make little changes at first: turning down a social engagement taking

you away from your family time. As you adjust, try other commitments.
"Plan. Make sure your goals are realistic. Reduce expenses and invest wisely to save money over time.

"Include family members. Let them offer their own priorities and work on changes together.

"Make sure it's your dream, not someone else's. 'Nuff said!

"Suggestions for around the house:

"Organize your kids' stuff with labels and envelopes kept in a box. Clean your kitchen floor by scooting wet paper towels around with your feet. Teach your kids basic math with baking."

Notes

CHAPTER FIVE

IRRIGATING AND WATERING

Source: *The Tennessee Master Gardener Handbook*, "Soil Water and Irrigation," H. Paul Denton

Water makes up more than 3/4 of the weight of green plants. Water is vital for many plant functions. It provides rigidity for the plant, transports food and nutrients, acts as a coolant, and is a raw material in many chemical reactions in the plant. Most plants can survive only a short time if there is no water available to them; they need water (either from what is stored in the ground, or from rain) every day. Lack of adequate water is the most common factor limiting plant growth in many lawn, garden, and farm situations.

Plants obtain water from the soil or growing media through their roots. Water is lost as vapor through openings in the leaf surface, called **transpiration** because of temperature, wind, and relative humidity. Temperature is by far the most important.

A lawn or garden with a full canopy cover (i.e. all the ground surface covered by plants) may use a third of an inch of water a day on a windy, clear, summer day with temperatures in the 90s. In the winter, when use is low, (in Tennessee) use is about .02 inches per day.

Water is also lost through evaporation from the soil surface, especially if it is bare and moist. The combination of water loss from plants and soil is called **evapotranspiration.**

In nature, water for plant growth comes from rainfall.

In Tennessee, the average rainfall is about 50 inches per year. The average annual evapotranspiration from a full canopy is about 30 inches per year. So, we have a surplus of about 20 inches going to groundwater or run off to streams. But rainfall may not occur for days or weeks at a time, and plants need water every day.

In the absence of irrigation, they draw from water stored in the rooting zone of the soil. During a prolonged dry period, the need for water may exceed that stored in the soil, and plants suffer from water stress. The likelihood of such stress depends on the amount of water the soil can store for plants. More than anything else, in the absence of irrigation, it is the amount of water a soil can store and provide back to plants that makes it a productive or unproductive soil.

A normal soil has about 50% pore space. After a heavy rain or irrigation, all this space may be filled by water and the soil is said to be **saturated.** This is not a desirable situation, as most plants need an aerated root zone. Fortunately, if there is no restriction of drainage, the force of gravity will remove water from the larger pores relatively quickly. After a saturated loamy soil is allowed to drain for 24 to 48 hours, the remaining water is held in the soil too tightly to be removed by gravity and drainage essentially ceases. This water content is called **field capacity**. Deep, silty, or loamy soils can store the most plant-available water, while shallow soils, sandy soils or gravelly soils store the least. Plants have to expend energy to absorb water, and the energy needed increases as the water content falls. For optimum growth, water content near field capacity is ideal.

Weeds use water just like desirable plants do. Controlling weeds through the season when they are small will help reduce total water use.

Mulches help reduce water loss from the soil surface

by evaporation. This is especially true if the plants are small or widely spaced, leaving much bare ground exposed to the sun. The reduced water loss improves uptake of nutrients and may help control some problems. Organic mulches improve infiltration of water from rainfall or sprinkler irrigation. Mulches also help in controlling weeds.

Of course, when rainfall is not enough, it will be important to use an irrigation system. Applying water to individual plants or small areas using a sprinkling can, garden hose or drip irrigation system will reduce the stress (wilting, twisting) before the plants begin to show those outward signs.

In hot weather, plants need 0.2 to 0.3 inches per day. Frequent shallow watering will encourage shallow root growth, so it is important to add 3/4 to 1 inch of water at one time. If you're using overhead sprinklers, the water must be added slowly enough for the soil to absorb it. Using a few small containers, spaced out over the area you are watering, will show you when you have added enough water. Using mulch to protect the surface will give a faster intake rate, but on most soils infiltration will not exceed 3/4 to one inch per hour.

The purpose of irrigation is to keep the effective root zone of the plant moist. As long as enough water is added to moisten the upper 6 to 8 inches of soil whenever it begins to get dry, that is really all that matters. The most common mistake in gardens is adding too little water too late. Observe the soil. If water is ponding on the surface and the soil is waterlogged for several hours after watering, too much is being added.

SPIRITUAL APPLICATION

God washes me with the cleansing water of His Word.

"Weathering the Showers," Beth Donigan Seversen.

"The Water Garden, by Claude Monet, is one of my favorite paintings. You will find the original in an impressionist museum, de l'Orangerie, in Paris. It is painted in the round and hangs in a circular room. When you stand in the center of the room you are completely engulfed in a luxuriant water garden!

"My print, hanging over the desk in my office, is only a small representation of the delightful, full-scale original. If you study the painting, one of the surprises you will find is that the major part of the canvas is covered in dark shades of black, blue and green. These rather drab colors stand in stark contrast to the delicate pastels. Actually, they serve to highlight the beautiful florals, which appear rich and striking upon the deep, dark waters. At first glance, your eyes are drawn to the colorful petals; then you realize that Monet painted the dark tones to enhance the lighter.

"Monet's painting has much to remind me about the water garden of my life, and of its Artist. First, it encourages me that there is a purpose and design to my life and that perhaps, at times, I focus too exclusively on the darker portions of my painting.

"It also reminds me that my Lord, the Artist of my life, has intentionally allowed the blue, green, and yes, sometimes even the gray and black hues to be brushed on my canvas for a reason. God uses these shadows to make my life richer. Often, when I look back on difficulties, such as my father's death, times when I have been misunderstood by friends, or my expectations have been dashed, I can see, now, His handiwork, creating a brilliance of color and beauty from pain and suffering. The Artist uses a multitude of techniques in our lives to help us become the people He created us to be.

"Finally, I am reminded that just like the water lilies in Monet's masterpiece, God keeps the leaves and petals afloat through the muck, wind, and rain that are part of the storms of life. Water gardens survive April showers and worse, and I will too, by God's help and grace."

We had a one-lane bridge on the road to one of our homes. One season the rains were so heavy, the creek rose, dragging with it fallen trees and lots of other debris against that bridge, washing out the road on each side so that no vehicle could cross. Now there was really not so much water that it couldn't flow <u>under</u> the bridge, but so much debris got in the way that the water had to go <u>over</u> the bridge, keeping anyone on foot from even jumping the gaps and walking across.

We get that way. We get clogged up with the debris

of anxieties, hurt feelings, envying (all lusts), physical problems, emotional problems, financial lack and the like–all that debris–and God's river can't flow through us.

How much easier it is to pull weeds after a rain. Some "things" in our lives (too much TV) can be a weed. It's easier to pull out spiritual weeds when God is "raining" on my life with understanding of His word.

What happens to a plant which is not watered? It dies. What happens to a person who does not receive the washing of the Word? (Ephesians. 5:25-26, "Husbands, love your wives, just as Christ loved the church and gave Himself up for her to make her holy, cleansing her by the washing with water through the word, and to present her to Himself as a radiant church, without stain or wrinkle or any other blemish, but holy and blameless, purifying her by His love and protection." As spiritual priest He "washes" His wife with the Word to make her spiritually clean. Divine love cleanses, cultivating purity, righteousness, and the sanctity of their wives.

The *McArthur New Testament Commentary on Ephesians*, Moody Press, develops these scriptures. "Love wants only the best for the one it loves, and it cannot bear for the loved one to be corrupted or misled by anything evil or harmful. When a husband's love for his wife is like Christ's love for His church, he will continually seek to purify her from any sort of defilement. He will seek to protect her from the world's contamination and protect her holiness, virtue, and purity in every way. He will never induce her to do that which is wrong or unwise, or expose her to that which is less than good."

Harper's Bible Dictionary, Harper Brothers Publishers, states that water is mentioned more frequently in scripture than any other natural resource.

-Jesus told the woman at the well about living water, meaning eternal life (John 4:13-14).

-Cup of water (Mark 9:41) describes Christian charity.

-"I planted, Apollos watered" (1 Corinthians 3:6) the seed of the church.

-"(the Son of man)...the sound of many waters." Revelation 1:11-15.

-Revelation 22 describes the river of the water of life.

-Matthew 3:6, baptism denotes the washing away of sin.

-Proverbs 11:25 says a generous person who waters others will himself be watered.

-Isaiah 44:3-5 LB promises, "I will give water to the thirsty land and make streams flow on the dry ground. I will pour out My Spirit on your children and blessing on your descendants. They will thrive like well-watered grass, like willows by steams of running water." Wow!

-Isaiah 58:11 LB, "I will always guide you and satisfy you with good things. I will keep you strong and well. You will be like a garden that has plenty of water, like a spring of water that never goes dry." Joy!

-Job 8:11-19 talks about the necessity for water in the life of a plant and likens it to all who forget God.

-Zechariah 14 states that on the coming day of the Lord (:8) living water will flow out from Jerusalem and it envisions God's blessings flowing from the millenial Jerusalem.

-2 Peter 2:1-17 regarding false teachers, calling them springs without water.

Other references: Psalms 126:5,6; Jeremiah 9:1; Jeremiah 14; and Jeremiah 31:16, refer to wayward children returning from the land of the enemy. Acts 20:19, 2 Corinthians 2:4, Nehemiah 8:9 (tears are a sign of the Holy Spirit's work). Note: Even today, those who weep in Christ are considered blessed. Revelation 7:17, Luke 7:38,

Psalm 56:8, Psalm 139:16, Matthew 6:25-30 (every tear shed by a faithful believer is treasured by God).

Charles Swindoll's *Growing Strong in the Seasons of Life*, Multnomah Press, includes a chapter titled "Tears" where he states (and I summarize): Tears are not self-conscious. Most often they appear when our soul is overwhelmed with feelings that words cannot describe. One of the great drawbacks of our cold, sophisticated society is its reluctance to show tears. The ultimate result is a well-guarded, highly respectable, uninvolved heart surrounded by heavy bars of confinement. Such a structure resembles a prison more than a home where the tender Spirit of Christ resides. How many (of the tear bottles in Heaven) bear *your* initials? You'll never have many until you impound restraint and let a little tenderness run loose. You might lose a little of your polished respectability, but you'll have a lot more freedom. And a lot less pride.

And he concludes: "When was the last time you cried? Have you ever cried alongside someone else as they experienced grief or joy? If you find yourself crying this week, don't try to hide the tears from those around you. Tears are beautiful to God! And to God's people."

Notes

CHAPTER SIX

MULCHING AND COMPOSTING

"Mulch, a loyal, true friend to the garden," by Diane Hellenman, *Gannet News Service.*

MULCHING

"Like any good friend, mulch need not be beautiful, but it should be loyal and hang around through stormy weather. It ought not to require lavish financial attention to become your friend or be hard to locate when you need it. Indeed, this true friend will not create problems in your life but help you solve them.

"Somehow we seem to be increasingly told that our old friends - shredded leaves, pine needles, newspaper, grass clippings, old raffia door mats and shredded bark - are not exactly the mulch one wants to be seen with in public.

"We need designer mulches, it seems, mulches with colors sprayed onto the wood in hues of Forest Green, Satin Black, Terracotta Orange, and Café au Lait.

"**Dressy mulch**

"Is it worth it or is it enhanced profit-margin

marketing that has nothing to do with real gardening? The latest blow is that they are now enhancing one of nature's best products by dyeing pine needles. According to *BioCycle Magazine*, colored mulches outsell old organic uncolored mulches five-to-one.

"Some gardeners have a few reservations about how colored wood mulches are produced. They are a by-product of waste wood such as pallets and building debris.

"Such recycling is a good idea, but for the gardener the issue is that the wood has not been composted, so it will reduce nitrogen in beds where it is used. The standard answer is to simply toss a handful of fertilizer here and there, however this doesn't sound like a friendly solution to me.

"Plus, there are other issues, such as dye leaching onto concrete driveways from stored mulch and fear that some building debris might have lead paint or asbestos in it, but I am sure our recycling industry would not pull such bad tricks upon its public.

"So, other than good looks, what do you want in your mulch friend? It should make your soil better and not render it incapable of supporting life.

"*Backyard Conservation*, U. S. Department of Agriculture, states that mulching is one of the simplest and most beneficial practices you can use in the garden. Mulch is simply a protective layer of a material that is spread on top of the soil. Mulches can either be organic–such as grass clippings, straw, bark chips, and similar materials–or inorganic–such as stones, brick chips, and plastic. Both organic and inorganic mulches have numerous benefits: protects the soil from erosion, reduces compaction from the impact of heavy rains, conserves moisture, reducing the need for frequent watering, maintains a more even soil temperature, prevents weed growth, keeps fruits and vegetables clean, keeps feet clean, allowing access to the garden even when damp, and provides a "finished" look to the garden. They also improve the condition of the soil. As these mulches slowly decompose, they provide organic matter which helps keep the soil loose. This improves root growth, increases the infiltration of water, and also improves the water-holding capacity of the soil. Organic matter is a source of plant nutrients and provides an ideal environment for earthworms and other beneficial organisms.

"**When to apply:** Time of application depends on what you hope to achieve by mulching. Mulches, by providing an insulating barrier between the soil and the air, moderate the soil temperature. This means that a mulched soil in the summer will be cooler than an adjacent unmulched soil; while in the winter, the mulched soil may not freeze as deeply. However, since mulch acts as an insulating layer, mulched soils tend to warm up more slowly in the spring and cool down more slowly in the fall than unmulched soils.

"If you are using mulches in your vegetable garden or flower garden, it is best to apply them after the soil has warmed up in the spring. Cool, wet soils tend to slow seed germination and increase the decay of seeds and seedlings.

"If adding additional layers of mulch to existing perennial beds, wait until the soil has warmed completely.

"Mulches used to help moderate winter temperatures can be applied late in the fall after the ground has frozen but before the coldest temperatures arrive. Applying mulches before the ground has frozen may attract rodents looking for a warm overwintering site. Delayed applications of mulch should prevent this problem as hopefully the creatures would already have found some other place to nest.

"Mulches used to protect plants over winter should be loose materials such as straw, hay, or pine boughs that will help insulate the plants without compacting under the weight of snow and ice. One of the benefits from winter applications of mulch is the reduction in the freezing and thawing of the soil in the late winter and early spring. These repeated cycles of freezing at night and then thawing in the warmth of the sun cause many small or shallow rooted plants to be heaved out of the soil. This leaves their root systems exposed and results in injury or death. Mulching helps prevent rapid fluctuations in soil temperature and reduces the chances of heaving.

"**Pine straw:** It can be pricey unless you are raking your own, but it is pretty, it locks in place, and it creates an airy barrier that avoids evaporation and heat buildup while retaining soil moisture. Despite the common "knowledge" that it will acidify the soil, recent studies suggest this is not really true.

"**Shredded bark:** Hard to beat this. Call the darker hardwood types "Coffee Grounds," and appreciate that they will last a year and slowly decompose to add humus. Call the lighter cypress back "Saratoga Shreds," and appreciate that it will last several years because it is resistant to decomposition, which makes it both good and bad for a gardener. The reason that cypress is so expensive is because it has to be hauled from Florida, so common sense might send you to hardwood bark used under the tougher cypress.

"**Tree trimmings:** A load of chipped trimmings from tree work in your area can be a wonderful assist if you have a spot where the pile can sit for six months or longer. Just like colored mulch, this wood is not decomposed and can cause nutrient deficiencies if used too soon.

"**Dry shredded leaves:** A make-at-home compost-mulch, this is usable straight as it is in the fall or can be stockpiled for later.
"**Newspaper:** A section of 12 pages laid on the mowed ground will smother weeds. Similar sections pieced around plants will create a degradable weed barrier. Always cover the flyaway paper with a heavier mulch. The inks are OK, but avoid the slick color pages, which don't break down and tend to get slimy.

"**Grass clippings:** These are fine to smother weeds in paths but tend to mat on the outside and get slimy on the inside if stacked very deep. The best use is to combine them in a compost pile and use that product later. You cannot use clippings from grass treated with an herbicide or a weed-and-feed product.

"**Marginal mulch (better-than-nothing)**

"**Plastic sheets:** Black plastic will warm up soil in early spring. It also overheats the ground in the summer, collects water for mosquito larvae and is pure waste you can't recycle. Red plastics, once touted as miracle growth enhancers for tomatoes, have proved more modest crop gains of 10 percent or less. It is, however, true that yellow plastic will attract whiteflies and other pests, which makes it easier for natural predators to eat them. Silver plastic discourages aphids, for whatever that is worth to the home gardener.

"**Landscape fabric weed barriers:** There might be one out that is great, but experience has been that they are difficult to handle, obnoxious to look at and do not degrade evenly.

"**Peat moss:** The texture is too fine to use for mulch. It will form a water barrier to rain.

"**Wood nuggets:** These always roll around and pop out of their appointed place, but they are popular.

"**Making much of your mulch**

"–Three inches will do. Too deep and the mulch has the potential to become water-soaked, truly acidic and "sour," which means toxic to your plants. Smell a bag of mulch before you buy it. It should not smell sour.

"–Fluff up mulch in the spring periodically. This, as much as anything, will help reduce build up of sow bugs and slugs that find mulch such a happy habitat.

"–Keep mulch six inches away from the stems of plants and at least six inches away from the trunks of trees to avoid pest problems.

"–Opt for mulch rather than turf under trees.

Trees grow better, and the mulch provides protection from mower damage.

"–Wait until perennials are up and growing before you mulch in the spring. Wait until the ground freezes to apply winter mulch.

"–Do not freak out about termites, which will not be attracted by the mulch but are probably hanging out in your yard eyeing dead trees and lumber piles.

"–Do not freak out over nuisance fungi; just stir up the mulch if you can't find it in your heart to be curious and compassionate about the life cycle of another living creature.

"–Do not fear a rustic look made by mixing in homemade compost or shredded dry leaves."

SPIRITUAL APPLICATION

God, in the form of the blessed Holy Spirit, is my protector, my covering.

Mulching is indicative of warmth, security, protection, nearness, a covering.

Jesus (Luke 13:34) lamented, "Oh Jerusalem, Jerusalem, how often have I longed to gather your children together, as a hen gathers her chicks under her wings, but you were not willing."

Boaz, to Ruth, referring to her unselfishness toward Naomi (Ruth 2:12), "May the Lord repay you for what you have done. May you be richly rewarded by the Lord, the God of Israel, under whose wings you have taken refuge."

David, to the Lord, when his enemies were pursuing him (Psalm 17:8). "Keep me as the apple of Your eye; hide me in the shadow of Your wings."

Generally regarding God's ways (Psalm 91:4), "He will cover you with His feathers and under His wings you will find refuge. His faithfulness will be your shield and rampart."

COMPOSTING

Source: *Backyard Conservation. It'll grow on you.*
U. S. Department of Agriculture

All organic matter eventually decomposes. Composting speeds the process by providing an ideal environment for bacteria and other decomposing microorganisms. The final product, humus or compost, looks and feels like fertile garden soil. This dark, crumbly, earthy-smelling stuff works wonders on all kinds of soil and provides vital nutrients to help plants grow and look better.

Decomposing microorganisms need four key elements to thrive: nitrogen, carbon, moisture, and oxygen. For best results, mix materials high in nitrogen (such as clover and fresh grass clippings) and those high in carbon (such as dried leaves and twigs). If there is not a good supply of nitrogen-rich material, a handful of general lawn fertilizer will help the nitrogen-carbon ratio. Moisture is provided by rain, but you may need to water or cover the pile to keep it damp. Be careful not to saturate the pile. Oxygen is supplied by turning or mixing the pile. More turning yields faster decomposition.

Many materials can be added to a compost pile, including leaves, grass clippings, straw, woody brush, vegetable and fruit scraps, coffee grounds, livestock manure, sawdust, and shredded paper. Avoid using diseased plants, meat scraps that may attract animals, and dog or cat manure which can carry disease.

Composting can be as simple or as involved as you would like, and depends on how much yard waste you have, how fast you want results, and the effort you're willing to invest.

With **cold composting**, you can just pile grass clippings and dry leaves on the ground or in a bin. This method requires no maintenance, but you'll have to wait several months to a year for the pile to decompose. Cold composting works well if you're short on time or have little yard waste. Keep weeds and diseased plants out of the mix. Add yard waste as it accumulates.

Hot composting requires more work, but with a few minutes a day and the right ingredients you can have finished compost in a few weeks. Hot piles must be built all at once in a 4-5 foot cube and turned regularly. As decomposition occurs, the pile will shrink. A 3 foot cube is needed to maintain necessary heat. Hot piles can reach 110 to 160 degrees Fahrenheit, killing most weed seeds and plant diseases.

On a level site, lay down bricks or prunings to promote air circulation. Spread several inches of the high-carbon material, then mix high-carbon and high-nitrogen material together. Water periodically. Punch holes in the sides of the pile for aeration. The pile will heat up and then begin to cool. Start turning when the pile's temperature begins to drop.

Move materials from the center to the outside and vice versa. Turn every day or two and you should get compost in less than 4 weeks. Turning every other week will give compost in 1 to 3 months. Finished compost will smell sweet and be cool and crumbly to the touch.

Compost bins may be as simple as a ventilated garbage can (poke holes all over it), wire mesh formed into a circle, picket fencing, pressure treated wood, brick or concrete blocks and, as we have done, pallets wired together standing up. My husband sunk a post behind each pallet on the outside to make the bin more stable.

Common problems. Composting is not an exact science. Experience will tell you what works best for you. If you notice that nothing is happening, you may need to add more nitrogen, water, or air. If things are too hot, you probably have too much nitrogen. Add some more carbon materials to reduce the heating. A bad smell may also indicate too much nitrogen.

Cold composting often proceeds faster in warmer climates than in cooler areas. Cold piles may take a year or more to decompose depending on the materials in the pile and the conditions.

Adding kitchen wastes to compost may attract flies and insects. To prevent this problem, make a hole in the center of your pile and bury the waste.

Using compost. Compost can be used for all your planting needs. Compost is an excellent source of organic matter to add to your garden or potted plants. It helps improve soil structure which contributes to good aeration and moisture-holding capacity.

Compost is a source of plant nutrients. Compost can also be used as a mulch material. Studies have shown that compost used as a mulch, or mixed with the top one inch layer of soil, can help prevent some plant diseases, including some of those that cause damping of seedlings.

On the farm, potential waste is turned into a resource that saves money and helps the environment. Producers use livestock manure to fertilize crops. When manure is properly handled, it can be safely applied to the land without the risk of polluting water. Composting is also practiced in some poultry operations. The compost is used as fertilizer on the farms and for lawns and gardens.

SPIRITUAL APPLICATION

What can we liken compost to spiritually? Could it be the dregs of our lives which we have given to the Lord, the experiences which have been good teachers, and the sinful behavior which we have overcome with the Lord's help? These certainly enrich our lives. We then comfort others with the comfort we have received (2 Corinthians 1:3-5), because we've been where they are. We wouldn't want to repeat many of the trials we've gone through, but we have been strengthened and enriched by them.

In the practical application, compost is formed as organic material dies and decomposes, creating a rich material to be added to beds. Wouldn't it be true then, that as my flesh dies to its desires my life is enriched?

Notes

CHAPTER SEVEN

PRUNING

Sources: *The Tennessee Master Gardener Handbook*, University of Tennessee Agricultural Services
Sunset Western Garden Book, Lane

The objective of pruning is to modify the plant's growth. It can be done to maintain plant health by removing dead, diseased or injured wood, to control or direct growth, or to increase quality or yield of flowers or fruit.

You never should have to cut back a plant continually to keep it in bounds. A plant that seems to require such treatment was the wrong choice for its garden location; the repeated cutting back only destroys the plant's natural beauty. Exceptions to this are formal hedges, espaliering fruit trees, and shaping topiary.

Since all growth originates in *buds*, they are the first parts to consider.

Terminal growth buds develop at the end of a stem or branch. This bud causes the stem to grow in length.

Lateral buds grow along the sides of stems and produce sideways growth, making a plant bushy.

When a plant is actively growing, terminal buds will add length to the stems. If you cut off or nip any growing terminal bud, the stem or branch stops growing. All pruning cuts, including pinching, should be made just above some growth–a growth bud, stem, or branch.

Pinching is taking out new growth before it becomes a stem. It makes young plants bushier. A good example is to remove the first flower bud on a marigold or zinnia before they have a chance to open, to cause the plant to branch out and become a bushier plant with many flowers.

If you want a plant to get taller, keep the side growth pinched back so the terminal bud on the main stem continues to get longer.

Heading back (or cutting back) stops growth that causes a plant to get taller by cutting off whatever height you want of growth already formed. You can do this to remove weak or unproductive wood, to cause growth in the direction you want it to take (or prevent growth from continuing in the wrong direction), to stimulate flower or fruit production by encouraging growth of wood that will produce it, to prevent wind or snow damage to very long or heavy branches, and sometimes to revitalize an old plant. Topping trees (cutting off high branches at one height) is never advised. It destroys the shape and weakens the tree with new growth which will not be strong for quite a while. It also can open the branches to disease and insect damage.

Thinning (or lacing) is removing entire branches or limbs. This will open up a plant or tree by removing old, unattractive or unproductive growth, weak or excess growth, or limbs that take away the beauty of the plant's natural shape. When a tree is laced, it is opened up so that wind can pass through the branches, and not cause damage by breaking off branches which are too close together.

Shearing, is what is done to formal hedges and topiary. No regard is given to cutting above growing points, etc.

Root pruning. Some plant life (wisteria is a good example) will send up new growth from underground root runners. They will give you "babies" all over the place! To prune those roots, use a shovel and cut down through the roots all around the outside root zone of the plant every season, to be sure you aren't going to have too large a "family" of that plant.

Pruning cuts, when done properly, maintain the beauty of the tree or plant. Make the cut just above some sort of growth (a bud or stem). Do not leave a stub because in time it will wither and die, decay and drop of, leaving an open patch of dead tissue. When the cut is made just above a growing point, *callus* tissue will begin to grow inward and cover the cut surface. Best cuts place the lowest part of the cut directly opposite and slightly above the upper side of the bud or branch which you are cutting back. If you are using a hood and blade pruner, be sure the blade is closest to the branch that will remain. If the hook and blade are reversed, a small stub will be left. Thicker limbs will need a pruning saw.

When to prune. Flowering shrubs will bloom either from new growth or from old wood, depending on the plant species. Most spring-flowering shrubs bloom from wood formed during the previous year. Wait until they have finished flowering before pruning them (or do some pruning by cutting flowers while they are in bud or bloom). (They will cheer you if used as cut flowers in a vase in your home.) Growth made after flowering will provide blooms for the next year. (Forsythia is an example.)

Prune roses after they have gone dormant (usually in January) to remove dead or weak stems. While they are growing, prune them whenever it is necessary to shape them while you remove spent blossoms to keep hips from forming, because the bush will stop flowering. The hips are a signal to go to sleep.

When pruning an apple or pear tree, prune away growth until you only have a central leader (one branch pointing up). Peaches, prune (pit fruit) need to be opened up without a central leader, to receive more sunlight. And remove any weeds that grow in the "canopy" zone (any area under the reach of the outside branches); they take nourishment the tree's roots need.

Do not attempt to prune a tree which is more than ten to fifteen feet tall. Consult a professional arborist who is trained and equipped to do the job safely. There is a web site to consult: www.isa-arbor.com.

Often, when a tree is cut off at the ground, for whatever reason, suckers will continue to sprout from the trunk that is in the ground, indicating that it is still alive. If the tree has been accidentally removed, a new tree can be allowed to grow from one of those suckers, choosing the most healthy-looking one (usually the largest and straightest), and training it as it grows. Never take off more than ½ of the bottom branches. The tree needs these to draw nourishment while it is getting bigger. (On our property, when the loggers were removing the scrub pines, they often cut down or knocked down hardwood trees which were in the way of the skidder which was used to push the downed trees into a pile for loading. Now most of these have sprouted healthy new trees which I have pruned and shaped and they are becoming a beautiful new "forest.")

If you do not want the tree, you can cut an X over the top of the sawed-off trunk, which will help it to die, or use a chemical available at nurseries to cause it to die. We have found, on our property, that the stumps from logged-off scrub pines have decayed after about two years and are disintegrating in the ground. (If the pieces which break off are significant enough, and soft enough, I run them through the chipper into the compost pile.)

PRUNING

Pruning is one of the most important cultural practices in the landscape. Rarely will one find a tree, shrub or vine that does not need some pruning each year. Proper pruning will help produce a more attractive, vigorous and well-formed plant. In many cases, flowering will increase.

Pruning stimulates new growth and development of the plant. Pruned plants develop new growth where cuts are made, unless a branch is cut back to a main stem. Correct pruning may add years to the usefulness of the plant.

Begin pruning when plants are young. Early pruning on shrubs will increase the branching structure near the ground and develop a more compact plant. Pruning young trees correctly will ensure a straight center leader and scaffold branching. Trees need to be pruned correctly as they grow to eliminate massive corrective pruning when they are mature.

Why Prune?

Pruning is a necessary practice to maintain healthy, vigorous plants of desirable shape and size. Pruning cuts should be made for a reason:

1) To maintain plant health by removing dead or diseased plant tissue. This is necessary to maintain the health and vigor of the plant. Make the pruning cuts into healthy tissue.

2) To remove branches that are misshaped, crowded, rubbing together or drooping onto other branches for support. Preventative maintenance involves removing such branches before injury occurs.

3) To stimulate or increase flowering or fruiting. Many flowering plants will produce more flower buds the following season, if old flowers are removed when they lose their attractiveness. A common phrase for this type pruning is dead heading.

4) To improve the appearance of the plant by training to a particular shape or size. Pruning can shape or train plants in unnatural forms such as hedges or espaliers.

5) To rejuvenate old, overgrown shrubs to restore their shape and vigor. When shrubs become overgrown, severe pruning is necessary.

This prevents plants, especially shrubs, from becoming overgrown and crowding or shading other plants.

Proper Pruning Techniques

If major pruning cuts are made every three years, the plant selected for the site is probably wrong. A common example is where potentially large hollies, privet or photinia are planted in front of picture windows. It does not take long for these plants to grow to the point the view from the window is obscured. When the plant is cut back or severe renewal pruning is done, the plant quickly grows back to its original size due to the large established root system.

There are many pruning styles for shrubs, but there are two basic pruning cuts: heading and thinning. Heading cuts often shorten a branch or stem; thinning cuts remove a branch at its base or where a side branch arises. Whether a shrub is sheared into a hedge or pruned with a natural growth habit, these two cuts are used.

Heading cuts are made just above the nodes (Figure 11). The buds directly below a heading cut generally produce new shoots. To encourage shoots to grow outward and produce a spreading

Figure 11. Proper pruning cuts.

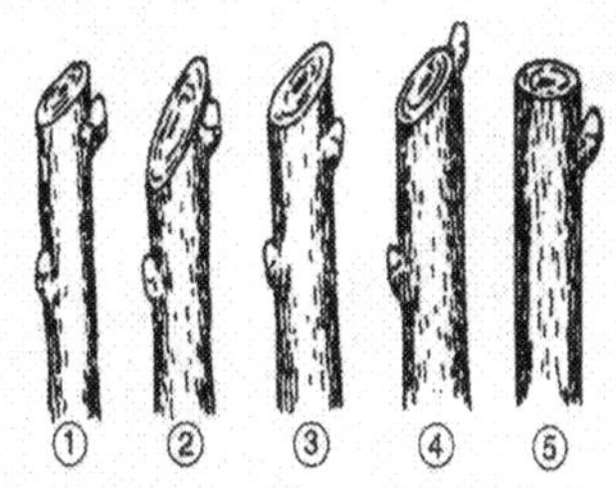

1. Good, bud safe from drying
2. Too slanting
3. Too far from bud
4. Too close to bud, bud may dry out
5. Stub may rot

shrub, cut above a bud facing outward. Buds that face inward may yield branches that are crowded and impair the anticipated growth form. Leave enough of a stub below the cut to keep the bud from drying out.

Cut plants that have opposite bud arrangement, 1/4 inch above the buds at a right angle to the stem. Usually, both buds will grow, producing two equal new shoots going in opposite directions, which is often undesirable. Rub or cut off the unwanted bud, probably the one facing inward. Maple, dogwoods and ash are common landscape trees that have opposite bud arrangement. It is difficult to maintain a center leader in these trees without diligent pruning.

Thinning

Some shrubs need thinning by cutting about one-third of the older branches back to the ground level every couple of years (Figure 12). This allows new shoots to grow with a potential to increase flowering. Cutting the tips of the new growth during the growing season is also beneficial. This pruning technique may be used for shrubs with a similar branching habit, such as forsythia, spiraea, weigela, mahonia, mockorange, nandina and eleagnus.

Figure 12. Correct and Incorrect way to prune branching shrubs.

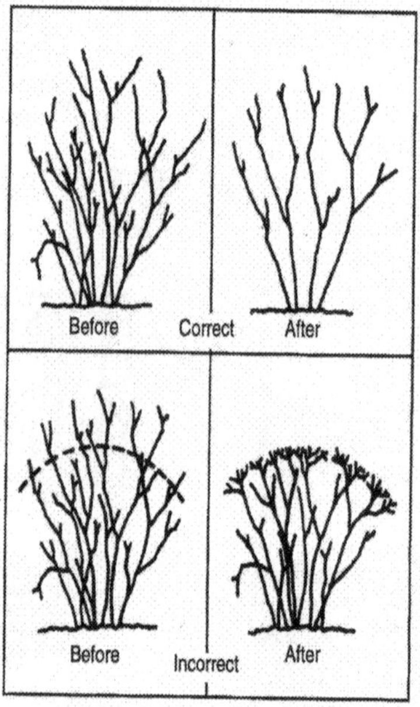

When To Prune?

Pruning can be done almost any time of the year, but there are optimal times for plant response. A plant's energy reserves are highest during the dormant period of winter and lowest during spring growth.
If pruning is during the action weeks of spring, the plant may draw on diminished reserves to replace at least part of the lost growth and to defend pruning wounds. Late summer and early fall are also poor times to prune, because this may encourage new growth that will not mature sufficiently to withstand winter freezes and may be killed by an early fall frost. Finally, avoid pruning in late fall or early winter; the wounds could stay open until spring, inviting dessication. An old rule is do not prune when the temperature is below 20° F.

The best time to prune is late winter or early spring, before buds start to swell and open. Plants have plenty of stored energy and are ready to grow. Dormant pruning may reduce the amount of flowering on shrubs that flower in spring, but occasionally it is necessary to maintain the desired growth form. Prune birch, elm, maple and yellowwood in late winter. Avoid pruning in early spring because these trees are prone to bleeding or sap release.

The next best time to prune is in early summer after all the foliage has matured. Wait for a day the foliage is dry, especially if diseases such as mildew or fire blight are evident. Use this pruning time as a method to control height or to develop a more dense shrub.

Trees and shrubs should be examined for pruning on an annual basis. Too many homeowners neglect their shrubs and fail to prune for several years. Shrubs become overgrown (a loss of vigor may occur) requiring heavy pruning or severe renewal pruning to reduce the size of the plant. Never hesitate to cut out tall, fast growing or unsightly limbs while they are growing. If the terminal bud is pinched or lightly pruned on new growth, lateral growth will occur and result in a fuller plant.

SPIRITUAL APPLICATION

The Lord keeps me in shape.

Women's Devotional New Testament, NIV, Zondervan. "**Divine Pruning.** What would you think if your best friend told you that she thought you needed to endure a long, intense, and difficult trial so that God could prune away some of the sin in your life? You would probably think she was crazy! What if she persisted and said that you would perform your job as a mother, wife, teacher or salesperson better after your trial was over? Which of us would willingly submit to those pruning shears, and which of us would turn, run and hide?

Jesus himself is the one who says that we need pruning: 'I am the true vine, and my Father is the gardener. He cuts off every branch in me that bears no fruit, while every branch that does bear fruit he prunes so that it will be even more fruitful...Neither can you bear fruit unless you remain in me.' John 15:1-2,4.

Here Jesus has issued warnings to all who profess to be believers. Unfruitful branches are those who confess Christ but never bear fruit, because they don't genuinely remain in him–they will be cut away. Fruitful branches, those who truly remain in Christ, will be pruned in order to bear more fruit for His glory.

When was the last time you felt 'pruned?' Perhaps it was when your invalid mother came to live with you, and suddenly your responsibilities and work load at home increased dramatically. Or maybe it was when your employer passed you over for promotion because he thought you weren't working hard enough.

Pruning is painful but profitable. James tells us that trials are occasions for joy because they will test our faith and develop in us perseverance and maturity (James 1:2-4).

We need God's help even to desire to yield ourselves to His pruning. May God bring people and events into our lives that will sanctify us so that we might bear true spiritual fruit for His glory and His kingdom's sake."

John 15:1-8 is a scriptural definition of the reason the Father prunes. My *Full Life Study Bible* has helpful commentary on these verses. "Jesus speaks of two categories of branches; fruitless and fruitful. The branches that cease to bear fruit are those which no longer have the life in them that comes from enduring faith in and love for Christ. These "branches" the Father cuts off, i.e., he separates them from vital union with Christ. (Matthew 3:10 warns "the ax is already at the root of the trees, and every tree that does not produce good fruit will be cut down and thrown into the fire.") When they stop remaining in Christ, God then judges and rejects them. The branches that bear fruit are those who have life in them because of their enduring faith in and love for Christ. These "branches" the Father prunes so that they will become more fruitful. That is, He removes from their lives anything that diverts or hinders the vital life-flow of Christ into them. The fruit is the quality of Christian character that brings glory to God through life and witness."

The text we just discussed stated that "the objective is to modify the plant's growth." And the reasons to prune were: "to maintain plant health by removing dead, diseased, or injured wood, to control or direct growth, and to increase the quality or yield of flowers or fruit."

Can you think of ways you've been pruned? Do you know why it was necessary?

When you're trying to cover too many bases you may not do anything as well as if you spent more time with a few more important issues; you're spread too thin. Fruit that is left becomes larger! It has spent more time with the tree. In Song of Solomon 1:6, the Shulammite maiden states that she has not tended her own garden because she's been too busy.

Every "plant/tree" has a predetermined, natural shape. You're unique. The Father knows what kind of "shape" you're supposed to have, and He'll remove any growth that obscures your basic pattern, or errant growth that departs from the natural form God intended you to have. Jeremiah 29:11-14 says, "I know the plans I have for you -----." The way the Lord prunes you will probably be very different from the way He prunes me.

In Rick Warren's book, *The Purpose Driven Life,* he has a chapter titled, "Shaped for Serving God." Some statements in this chapter are, "You were shaped to serve God." "You are a custom-designed, one-of-a-kind, original masterpiece."

He uses the acrostic **SHAPE**: **S**piritual gifts, **H**eart, **A**bilities, **P**ersonality, **E**xperience, to show what the Lord puts in each of our designs of uniqueness. He cited a study which revealed that the average person possesses from 500 to 700 different skills and abilities: your brain can store 100 trillion facts, your mind can handle 15,000 decisions a second, your nose can smell up to 10,000 different odors, your touch can detect an item 1/25,000th of an inch thick, and your tongue can taste one part of quinine in 2 million parts of water!! Wow! Psalm 139:14 says I am fearfully and wonderfully made, and this surely proves it!!

He sums up this chapter by stating, "God intentionally allows you to go through painful experiences (pruning) to equip you for ministry to others."

Have you ever wondered what a tree or bush might "say" while they are being pruned? "What are you doing!!" "Why are you treating me this way?" Sound familiar? I've sure asked questions like that!

Pastor Warren states, "Experience is not what happens to you. It is what you do with what happens to you. Don't waste your pain; use it to help others."

In another chapter he says, "The development of Christlike character cannot be rushed. Spiritual growth, like physical growth, takes time." And, I might add, it needs to be properly shaped. He adds, "While we worry about *how fast* we grow, God is concerned about *how strong* we grow." And He's pruning out whatever weakens our character. That can be painful.

When deadheading roses, this job is done to keep hips from forming and causing the bush to "think" it's time to go dormant and to stop flowering. How about retirement? Don't think your life is over, and it's time to "stop flowering" for the Lord. You don't retire, you **refire**!!

Here's a point to ponder: Will you be able to let go of your children when it's time for them to "leave"? Will you allow the Lord to "prune" them from you? (Genesis 2:24 says our children, when they marry, are to leave father and mother and cleave to each other and become one flesh.)

From *The Prophet* by Khalil Gibran, "On Children." "Your children are not your children. They are the sons and daughters of life's longing for itself. They come through you but not from you, and though they are with you, yet they belong not to you. You may give them your love, but not your thoughts. For they have their own thoughts. You may house their bodies, but not their souls, for their souls dwell in the house of tomorrow, which you cannot visit, not even in your dreams. You may strive to be like them, but seek not to make them like you. For life goes not backward nor tarries with yesterday. You are the bows from which your children as living arrows are sent forth. The archer sees the mark upon the path of the infinite, and he bends you to his might that his arrows may go swift and far. Let your bending in the archer's hand be for gladness; for even as he loves the arrow that flies, so he loves also the bow that is stable."

I found a little book at Wal-Mart, *What I Learned From God While Gardening,* by Niki Anderson and Cristine Bolley, Barbour Publishing. It's mostly a devotional, and I've found it to be very insightful. There's a chapter, "The Cutting Edge," which really fits into this study on pruning, and they start with the same John 15 scripture.

> "One spring I grew impatient for my husband to dig out a shrub. Disenchanted with the misshapen climber, I decided something different would be preferable in that spot. I grabbed my shears on an impulse and amputated every stem at ground level.
>
> "Summer progressed, and the barely visible evergreen bittersweet was forgotten. Much to my surprise, though, my radical pruning was not fatal. The hardy shrub was neither daunted nor stunted. By fall, new growth testified to its livelihood. The following spring I trained its new branches in graceful arches up to the chimney.
>
> "The experience with my shrub reminds me of a painful episode in my life as a young missionary in Africa. After battling malaria for fourteen months while teaching in Kenya, I reluctantly conceded to broken health and returned to the United States. My debilitating illness and an assault on my faith leveled me.
>
> "I was confused over God's intentions. Seized often by nausea, I also wrestled with the challenge of recurring attacks of malaria. My dismay over the curtailment of a life goal

buffeted me. I felt like a razed shrub.

"But in God's time, I experienced a renewal that matched the recovery of my shrub. The cycle of revival in the plant world is symbolic. It reminds us of the promise of resurrection that awaits in a coming season.

"Words from the Book of Job became my emotional lattice, and my healing began: 'There is hope of a tree, if it be cut down, that it will sprout again, and that the tender branch thereof will not cease.' (14:7)

"Emotional and physical recovery are sometimes as gradual as the slow unfurling of a tiny new leaf, but the love of parents, the counsel of ministers, the care of physicians, and months of rest healed my brokenness. One day I realized I was sprouting! Tender shoots of joy, faith and physical strength had grown under the sunshine of God's faithfulness. It was springtime once again!

"Gardeners realize the value of reshaping, retraining, and controlling the contours of a plant. Can we not then trust God when He clips away at us with divine secateurs (pruning shears)? He intends only to enhance those whom He prunes. How much more will we flourish when we are sheared by the expert skills of the Master Gardener!

"Thank you, God, for roots that keep me anchored when You prune my wayward limbs."

Using the cutoff stumps on our property as an example, many of the stumps continue to send out suckers, indicating that though the tree has been eliminated, the roots are not dead. We must be very studious in examining our "garden," making sure the roots have been pruned out so that old habits and sinful behaviors don't continue to "sucker."

Charles Swindoll, *Growing Strong in the Seasons of Life*, Multnomah Press, in a chapter titled "Habits," gave his own experiences with nail biting, indicating the habit caused him personal embarrassment and physical limitations, and cited 1 Corinthians 6:12, "All things are lawful for me, but not all things are profitable. All things are lawful for me, but I will not be mastered by anything."

Quoting him, "Not a person who reads this book is completely free from bad habits, whether lawless or lawful. That's the price we pay for being human. Some are wrestling with a habit as accepted and common as overeating or exaggerating or cheating or procrastinating. Others, by habit, are negative and suspicious, resulting in habitually closed-minded responses. While some are ungrateful and demanding, others are continually extravagant and undiscerning.

"Habits like gossip, worry, irritability, and profanity are often practiced without guilt, justified through cleverly devised mental schemes. The list is endless, for habits are as numerous as every detail of life."

Let the Lord "prune" out those habits by being honest about them and allowing His pruners to go to work. Maybe they only need "pinching" to stop the bud from developing before you are ready to "branch out" and have the maturity of overcoming the habit and growing an abundance of flowers of ministry.

Maybe you need a little "heading back" to stop you from going in the wrong direction.

Thinning out unbelief can keep you strong when the winds of adversity are blowing.

If the Lord has a "shape" for you in an area of positional ministry, then He may shear your growth very distinctly.

Whatever pruning the Lord needs to do, remember, He will do it for your good (Romans 8:28, 1 Thessalonians 5:18), and you will have a beautiful, unique shape that will be pleasing to Him. (How's that for spiritual gymnastics?!)

Remember, in Song of Solomon 1:6, the Shulamite maiden said, "I have not tended my own garden." Keep a close eye on the shape you're in. The Lord may need to do some pruning!!

Notes

God's Garden

<u>CHAPTER EIGHT</u>

TOOLS AND EQUIPMENT

<u>Source:</u> *Dirt Cheap Gardening* by Rhonda M. Hart, Storey Communications, Inc.

Some tips from Jerry Baker (*America's Master Gardener,* The Yarden Care Company):

On all of your long-handled tools, mark off, by the inch, from the top to the bottom, with a file. Then use stain or ink in the file mark so that you always have a measuring device handy.

Always paint part of the lower handle and the top of the steel of your tools with a combination of color stripes to identify them as yours. That way, when they walk over to your neighbor's garage, you'll be able to identify them. It also makes them easier to find when you lay them down in the grass.

Keep all of the blades and points sharp with a file.

Cover all sharp edges with small pieces of old garden hose that have been slit to fit over the blades or tips when you are storing your tools.

Never put any of your tools away dirty. Wash and dry them, and then lightly spray with either WD-40 or Pam. (You can also keep a 5 gallon can of sand handy and dump into it the used oil when changing your vehicle's oil at home. Push your tool down in that to clean it off and oil it at the same time.)

The stirrup, or hula, hoe is great. Because it is sharp on both sides of the stirrup, I can eliminate weeds or loosen soil either by pushing or whacking!

God's Garden

A very good book (and tool) I've used a lot since coming back to Tennessee, is *The Southern Living Garden Book*, published by Oxmoor House. The publication has beautiful pictures of southern-growing gardens and plants.

Its introduction states: "The Spirit of Southern Gardening, what makes a garden southern? It's more than geographical location; it's more than a practiced style. True Southernness grows from a fervent quest for continuity–an instinctive recognition that the seeds we sow and the bulbs we share tell the world who we are and where we've been.

"One hundred years ago, the majority of Southerners earned their living from the land. Farmers belonged to a noble, honored profession and were lauded by Thomas Jefferson as 'the chosen people of God.' Their beliefs, values, and practices shape our gardens still."

SPIRITUAL APPLICATION

God's Word is a lamp and a light to keep me on track.

You can't cook a meal, repair a vehicle, construct a house, or tend a garden without tools. And when you have those tools, you can't do the job properly unless you know how to use them. When you know how to use them, they're no good sitting on the shelf or lying in a drawer. They're no good if they're rusty, dull, or broken. They can't help you if they're still in the box or bag in which you brought them home. You will have an awkward time using a left-handed tool if you're right-handed.

The Lord has also provided all kinds of useful tools for us to use. We have to use them properly and consistently. We can't properly apply scripture taken out of context. It has to be used as the Lord intended when He inspired the writer to record it.

Additional tools for Christian growth:

Submission. James 4:7-10, "Submit to God, He will come near to you."
1 Peter 2:13-15, "Submit to human authority, silencing ignorant talk of foolish people by the good things you do."

Giving. Mark 10:21, "You will have riches in Heaven."
Luke 6:30-31, "Do what you want done for you."

Serving. Psalm 100:2, "Serve the Lord with gladness."
Galatians 5:13, "Serve one another."

Forgiveness.

Matthew 6:15, "Forgive others so you will be forgiven." Forgiveness costs you your pride. Your self-will dies. It costs you the right to accuse those you hold unforgiveness toward. Jesus taught us how to forgive as He hung on the Cross and forgave those who put Him there. He said they did not know what they were doing. He recognized they were controlled by the enemy.

Discipline.

Of being available to serve others in the name of the Lord and for a testimony of His love.
Matthew 14:13-14, Matthew 15:32, Matthew 20:34.
Of being in church and involved in its activities; joined in fellowship with a specific body of believers. Hebrews 10:25.
Of being a good steward of all material possessions the Lord has allowed me to use. Luke 16:10-12.
Of caring for my own body, home, marriage, children, spouse, friends. Ephesians 5 and 6.
Of being salt and light in my world as a witness, giving my testimony, and by my actions. Matthew 5:13.

Prayer.

Quoting again from *Hayford's Bible Handbook*, the commentary states, "Prayer should not be thought of as a mystical experience in which people lose their identity in the infinite reality. Effective prayer must be a scripturally informed response of persons saved by grace to the living God who can hear and answer on the basis of Christ's payment of the penalty which sinners deserved. Prayer involves several important aspects: faith, worship, confession, adoration, praise, thanksgiving."

From the same commentary, "The Lord's prayer (often called the disciples' prayer) of Matthew 6:9-13, is an outline with seven major topics, each representing basic human need. This is the tool that teaches us how to pray.

1. The paternal need: 'our Father' verse 9. When you pray, all needs are met by the benevolence of a loving Father.
2. God's presence: 'Hallowed be Your name' verse 9. Enter His presence through praise (Psalm 100:4) and call Him 'Father' because of Christ's atoning blood (Hebrews 10:19-22; Galatians 4:4-6).
3. God's priorities: 'Your kingdom come' verse 10. Declare that His kingdom priorities (Romans 14:17) shall be established in yourself, your loved ones, your church, and your nation.
4. God's provision: 'Give us' verse 11. Jesus, the need-meeter, told us to pray daily, asking Him to supply all our needs.
5. God's forgiveness: 'and forgive us' verse 12. You need God's forgiveness, and you need to forgive others. Daily set your will to walk in love and forgiveness.
6. Power over Satan: 'and do not lead us...deliver us from the evil one' vs. 13. Pray a hedge of protection about yourself and your loved ones (Job 1:9-10, Psalm 91), and verbally put on the armor of God (Ephesians 6:14-18).
7. Divine partnership: 'for Yours is the kingdom,' verse 13. Praise God for sharing His kingdom, power, and glory with you (2 Timothy 4:18, Luke 10:19)."

The Lord provides tools of war(fare) also: 2 Corinthians 10:4. He tells us they are not carnal weapons, though. They are not flesh and blood. They are "mighty through God to the pulling down of strongholds." There are strongholds in our lives which only the spirit of the Lord can do away with, with our permission. We must be willing to recognize them and want them to be destroyed before they can be eliminated. Examples may include smoking, lying, gross exaggerations, pride, anger, bitterness, impatience, lust, self-focus, low self-esteem, fear, worry, anxiety, and procrastination.

Other scriptures which I have found to be excellent "tools" when praying are: Psalm 23 and the prayer of Jabez, 1 Chronicles 4:10. Last year I began using the prayer of Jabez as a model for my own praying, and believe that the opportunities I have had to teach this gardening Bible study are a result of asking the Lord to enlarge my territory.

Psalm 91 is a model to use when fear would try to grip you. Many years ago, when I was a single mom, and I was alone in my home, using this Psalm and Isaiah 32:18, ("My people will live in peaceful dwelling places, in secure homes, in undisturbed places of rest,") gave me peace. Psalm 34:7, ("The angel of the Lord encamps around those who fear Him, and He delivers them,") was another one I prayed back to the Lord, reminding Him of His promise of safety.

Colossians 1:9-12 is one of four prayers, spoken by the Apostle Paul, where you can enter the name of someone you are praying for, and it guides you in powerful prayer for them. The *Full Life Study Bible* has commentary regarding these four prayers, "This (Colossians 1:9-12) is one of Paul's four great New Testament apostolic prayers, spoken under the inspiration of the Spirit (Ephesians 1:16-19, 3:14-19, and Philippians 1:9-11 are the other three).

"From these prayers we learn how to pray for others, such as our children, friends, fellow believers, missionaries, pastors, etc. We must pray that they may (1) understand God's will, (2) gain spiritual wisdom, (3) live holy lives pleasing to the Lord, (4) bear fruit for Christ, (5) be strengthened spiritually by the Holy Spirit, (6) persevere in faith and righteousness, (7) give thanks to the Father, (8) continue in the hope of heaven, (9) experience Christ's nearness, (10) know Christ's love, (11) be filled with God's fullness, (12) show love and kindness to others, (13) discern evil (14) be sincere and blameless, and (15) eagerly await the Lord's return."

It continues, referring to verse 11, "In order to live in a manner worthy of the Lord (verse 10) we must be strengthened by His power. This impartation of power is an ongoing experience of receiving from God His own life. Nothing else can enable us to overcome sin, Satan, and the world. (Philippians 4:13, "I can do everything through Him who gives me strength.")

As mentioned in the text about knowing how to use gardening tools, the same is true in relation to the "tools" the Lord gives us. Remember David and Saul's armor? David didn't want to wear it because he "wasn't used to it" (GNB). He could only be skillful with the slingshot because that was what he had used to kill the enemies of his sheep, as a shepherd. Learn the Word of God and be skillful in its application. Then, become like a hoe which has no value until the gardener uses it. You cannot do His work unless you let Him flow though you. You become His tool. But remember: you must be clean, sharp and well-oiled!!

THE KEY

There is a key called tenderness
That opens wide the door
That had been shut from some event
Not understood before.
Go try the key, unlock the door
With a forgiving smile.
For learning how to use the key

God's Garden

Can make a life worthwhile.
-Anonymous

Books which can help in Bible study:

Strong's Exhaustive Concordance of the Bible by Abingdon Press
Hayford's Bible Handbook, Jack Hayford, Thomas Nelson Publishers
Everyone in the Bible, William P. Barker, Fleming H. Revell Company
Atlas of the Bible, Reader's Digest
Bible Life & Times, Reader's Digest.

I've read the Bible through in many translations: *King James, New King James, New International Version, Living Bible, Amplified, Full Life Study Bible* (which is NIV), *Good News, New American Standard, New Testament in Modern English* by J. B. Phillips (often referred to as the Phillips's translation), and right now I'm using *The Bible for Today's Christian Woman* in the Contemporary English Version, by Thomas Nelson Publishers. Reading from many different translations will give you a better understanding of the scriptures for application to your own lives, not just memorizing them in one translation.

Other translations include: *God's Word Translation, The Message, New American Bible, New Century Version, New Jerusalem Bible,* and *New Living Translation.*

Notes

CHAPTER NINE

CLOTHING

A well-dressed gardener won't be too "fashionable" when working outside. You're going to be working pretty hard, most of the time, and you should try to be as comfortable, and safe, as you can.

A large-brimmed hat is a must. Be stylish! Not only will it make you look like a real gardener (!), it will protect you from the sun, and if the brim is wide enough, keep a lot of the sun off your neck besides.

Sun screen is <u>very</u> important. You should use SPF above 20 with UVA and UVB protection. It should be waterproof because you'll sweat it off. Coppertone Sport is a good example of one that will give you good protection.

I couldn't get along without my kneepads. Kneeling is much better for your back, but on cold, hard, wet, or rocky ground you need pads to cushion your knees. I found some inexpensive ones which fasten with velcro.

I strongly advise you <u>not</u> to garden in flip-flops, clogs, or other loose-fitting shoes; it's just too easy to fall or walk out of them when you're so active. And wear socks to keep your feet cleaner and protect from (some!) bug bites. Comfortable tennis shoes with arch supports, or proper fitting boots will be better for your feet and your back, with all the walking, bending and lifting, and whatever else you'll be doing. (Gardening is great exercise!)

It is important to protect your hands from scratches, cuts, and soil-borne bacteria. Because our area has predominantly been agricultural, there is a danger of e-coli bacteria in the soil. So be sure to wear gloves: goat skin is soft and strong, and there are gloves now which have knit (ventilated) backs and rubberized palms which make them more comfortable for warmer weather gardening.

Because we are in a "buggy" area, protect your legs, arms, face and neck with a repellent with Deet (like Off). I use the Deep Woods Off. Do not wear any kind of cologne or scented lotion. The scent will draw bugs to you.

Some gardening catalogs carry protective netting "jackets" which also cover the face. I've not used one, but there are times when I haven't applied Off that I wished I'd had one on.

Long pants (sometimes with the bottoms tucked inside your socks) will give better protection to your legs, as will long sleeves, but boy, you soon pass the "glowing" stage and start to just plain sweat when you're covered up so much! That's okay, as long as you drink plenty of water. I carry a ½ gallon-sized thermos with water when I'm working out for a while. I usually drain it.

Garden Gate Magazine. June, 2001. "Hands and gloves."

> "You know, there's something satisfying about working in the garden with bare hands. You can carefully untangle each root you plant and feel the grain of the wood on your trowel's handle as you dig. I even like finding a worm in a handful of soil. For some jobs, such as transplanting seedlings, gloves can be downright clumsy. But there are times when they come in handy, not to mention *healthy*.
>
> **"Why protect your hands?**
>
> "How many times have you thought, "I'll just snip this one unruly rose cane," only to find yourself 20 minutes later up to your elbows

in canes - and ultimately covered in scratches? If only you'd taken the time to find your gloves. This is why I like to keep mine handy.

"And say your hands already have nicks and scratches. The soil is filled with bacteria, good and bad. Most of the time it doesn't affect you. But if you have an open sore on your hand, exposure to some bacteria could lead to infection. Keep an eye on scratches and cover them with a bandage before you work in the garden, even with gloves. If they start to look angry, use some antibacterial cream or ointment.

"You may have heard of an even scarier bacteria–the 'flesh-eating bacteria.' In fact, it does exist in the soil. The good news is it usually only attacks through a deep puncture wound–a scratch probably isn't a deep enough entry point. However, if you have a sore that quickly becomes painful, swollen or develops pockets of air under the skin around it, contact your physician immediately.

"If you're working with chemicals, it's also a good idea to protect your skin–but with something more than your usual garden gloves. You just don't know what you may be exposing yourself to–burns, rashes, or maybe worse, in the long run.

"Choosing gloves

"Now that you know when and why to protect

yourself, how do you choose your gloves? I like mine to offer maximum protection and to fit snugly, so I usually wear leather gloves.

"Cotton is also good for protecting your hands. It gets wetter faster than leather and doesn't offer quite the resistance against snags that leather does. But it's inexpensive, cooler, and the gloves are easier to get on and off.

"When you're working with chemicals, leather and cotton can soak up liquid and powdered chemicals. So a pair of disposable rubber gloves is a must. This way you get rid of them as soon as you've finished spraying, and you minimize your exposure.

"Have you ever dug a hole and uncovered shards of glass or rusty nails? Me too. (I keep waiting for something valuable, like a diamond ring, to turn up!) It's a good idea to protect yourself with an up-to-date tetanus shot. This way, if you do get scratched by a nail, you won't have to worry; just wash up and move on.

"Clean up

"This brings me to another point. Always wash your hands after working in the garden, even if they don't *look* dirty. One thing I like to do is keep a bar of soap and a scrub brush handy by my outdoor faucet.

"One other by-product of working with soil is

that you end up with dry hands. Why? Well, the soil is like a sponge: It craves moisture and will take it wherever it finds it, even if it's from your skin. And all that washing up only exacerbates the issue. So once you've washed, make sure to use a good lotion right away. When your skin is still damp, it absorbs the lotion better. Work it into your cuticles and knuckles, as these are the areas that bear the brunt of the damage.

"Once you find gloves that you like, buy a couple of pairs so you can keep them handy all the time. You never know when you might need them. Have a pair in the car, a pair in your pocket, a pair in the shed – you know how it is!"

SPIRITUAL APPLICATION

I am clothed in His righteousness.

Erma Bombeck wrote, *Don't Show up for the New Year Overdressed.*

> "For years, I've studied the symbol of New Year's. . . a smiling baby wearing a diaper and a top hat. What does it mean? A beginning of life? A time of innocence? A scenario for change? Then it hit me. For years, I've been overdressed for the new year.
>
> "I enter it with shoulders bent, swathed in all the ills of the previous year, and when I can't wear them all on my body, I lug them along in heavy boxes and suitcases, kicking them along with my foot to make sure all of them make it into the next year of my life.
>
> "Wrapped around my neck is a mantle of guilt, some of it going back as far as 1940. (Guilt for the time my parents gave me a savings bond for my high school graduation when I wanted a silver charm bracelet, and I threw the savings bond on the floor. An oldie, but a goodie.)
>
> "The shirt of self-pity is uncomfortable, but for years it has provided me with enough ammunition to bring tears to the eyes of my husband and children. To discard it would be unthinkable. After all, self-pity, if you do it

right, takes a long time to amass.

"The belt of prejudice is an old one and encompasses anyone who does not agree with every single word I have ever said.

"The large footlocker contains anger. True, a lot of it doesn't fit anymore, but I hang onto it just in case I'm caught short.

"Adorning all of this are the jewels of frustration over things that I can never do anything about, but which I wear like medals to torture myself.

"And of course, the biggest piece of baggage contains old grudges that I sift through each year like old photographs and pressed flowers...the critic who was unkind...the trust that was abused by a child...the harsh words from a family member that I refuse to forget. Grudges, many of them antiques, that I plan on handing down to my children.

"Each year of my life, the load gets heavier and heavier to carry into a new year.

"Frankly, I don't know if I can face a new year without my clothes on. I don't know if I can check in without luggage. Can I look at old friends and see them for the first time? Can I keep my eyes forward and not look back? Do I have the guts to emerge with nothing on but a smile and a top hat? I'm going to try."

The scriptures have a lot to say about clothing, and so many of those scriptures imply, "you dress yourself!"

Romans 13:14. "Clothe yourselves with the Lord Jesus Christ, and do not think about how to gratify the desires of the sinful nature."

Colossians 3:12. "Therefore, as God's chosen people, holy and dearly loved, clothe yourselves with compassion, kindness, humility, gentleness and patience."

1 Peter 5:5. "Young men, in the same way be submissive to those who are older. All of you clothe yourselves with humility toward one another, because God opposes the proud, but gives grace to the humble."

From *Women's Devotional Bible, Daily Devotions from Godly Women*, Zondervan, June 28, "To reverence God requires a certain courage, because honestly facing up to who God is makes me face up to who I am. The more I see of God's holiness, the more I see my lack of it. Some call this 'humility,' but whatever name, it is simply facing up to the facts about who God is, and in that light, who I am."

Job 29:14. "I put on righteousness as my clothing; justice was my robe and my turban."

Matthew 7:15. "Watch out for false prophets. They come to you in sheep's clothing, but inwardly they are ferocious wolves."

Isaiah 61:3 NIV. "(the Lord---has sent me to) provide for those who grieve in Zion – to bestow on them a crown of beauty instead of ashes, the oil of gladness instead of mourning, and a garment of praise instead of a spirit of despair." And verse 10 CEV, "I celebrate and shout because of my Lord God; His saving power and justice are the very clothes I wear. They are more beautiful than the jewelry worn by a bride or a groom."

Zechariah 3:3-5. "Now Joshua was dressed in filthy clothes as he stood before the Angel. The Angel said to those who were standing before Him, 'Take off his filthy clothes.' Then He said to Joshua, 'See, I have taken away your sin, and I will put rich garments on you.' Then I said, 'Put a clean turban on his head.' So they put a clean turban on his head and clothed him, while the Angel of the Lord stood by." What a description of what happens to us when we accept Christ as Savior!

Proverbs 31:22. "---she is clothed in fine linen and purple (royalty)." And verse 25. "She is clothed with strength and dignity."

The most protective clothing that we must wear is the armor of God, Ephesians 6:11-18 GNB. "Put on all the armor that God gives you so that you will be able to stand up against the Devil's evil tricks. For we are not fighting against human beings but against the wicked spiritual forces in the heavenly world, the rulers, authorities, and cosmic powers of this dark age. So put on God's armor now! Then when the evil day comes, you will be able to resist the enemy's attacks; and after fighting to the end, you will still hold your ground. So stand ready, with truth as a belt tight around your waist, with righteousness as your breastplate, and as your shoes the readiness to announce the Good News of peace. At all times carry faith as a shield; for with it you will be able to put out all the burning arrows shot by the Evil One. And accept salvation as a helmet, and the word of God as the sword which the Spirit gives you. Do all this in prayer, asking for God's help. Pray on every occasion, as the Spirit leads. For this reason keep alert and never give up; pray always for all God's people."

In 1979 I made this journal entry. "As I was sorting out my clothes, discarding items I was tired of, or didn't feel comfortable in, my purpose was to make room for a new wardrobe that I had prayed for.

> "Many things didn't fit well; I had 'outgrown' them; they were unattractive on me, and I had

kept them, thinking I should, because I needed them.

"Then the Lord started to deal with me about my 'spiritual' wardrobe.

"You know, we have our personal traits and characteristics that fill our 'wardrobe' and take up room, and when we 'wear' them we are uncomfortable, or we know they make us look 'unattractive.' But for lack of something better, we let them stay. We say, 'That's the way He made me;' or 'That's the way I am;' or 'That's just me.'

"But the Lord would have us discard these items and allow Him, through His Holy Spirit, to re-clothe us–give us a new 'wardrobe.' One that fits our 'maturing' figure. One that compliments our new image in Him.

"As you mature physically your hair color changes, and then your skin colors change, too. Different colors look better on you. You need to change your makeup. As your body matures, it's contours change (after 40 you fill out [or in] new areas!). Can you apply that spiritually – as you mature?

"Have you ever noticed the 'glow' on the face of one who basks in Jesus' presence?

"Have you ever seen a new beauty in someone after they've met the Lord?

"Lord, help me to be willing to 'weed' out my wardrobe.' Satan, you cannot put fear on me that I'll have 'nothing to wear' – be a 'nothing.'

"Lord, give me a new wardrobe. Clothe me with the garment of praise for the spirit of heaviness (Isaiah 61:3). Show me how to put on the armor for spiritual warfare (Ephesians 6:11-18). Clothe me in humility (Colossians 3:12). Show me how to put on a meek and quiet spirit (1 Peter 3:4). Put within my heart a melody; on my lips a song.

"Help me to discard that 'old man' and put in my 'closet' that 'new man' who is renewed daily (2 Corinthians 4:16).

"Make me teachable in Your ways, Lord. Let me be a city, set on a hill–a candle that is not hid under a bushel (Matthew 5:14)."

What kind of clothing is in your closet?

THE TOTAL WOMAN

The total woman is renewed daily (2 Corinthians 4:16) by the Word. She knows His Word is a lamp to her feet, and a light to her path (Psalm 119-105). She is careful (anxious) for nothing, but in everything in prayer and supplication with thanksgiving lets her requests be made known. And the peace which passes all understanding keeps her heart and mind through Christ Jesus (Philippians 4:6-7). She prays always with all prayer and supplication in the Spirit (Ephesians 6:18).

When she dresses she puts on the Lord Jesus Christ (Romans 13:14) and the whole armor of God, that she may be able to stand against the wiles of the devil. Taking to her the whole armor of God, that she may be able to withstand in the evil day, and having done all to stand. Standing therefore, having her loins girded about with truth, and having on the breastplate of righteousness; and her feet shod with the preparation of the gospel of peace; and above all taking the shield of faith, wherewith she shall be able to quench all the fiery darts of the wicked. And taking the helmet of salvation, and the sword of the Spirit, which is the word of God, she adorns herself with a meek and quiet spirit (Ephesians 6:11,13-17 and 1 Peter 3:4).

She knows how to minister to her family (Ephesians 5:22 Amp). As a wife, she is subject and submissive and adapts herself to her own husband as a service to the Lord. She respects and reverences her husband, notices him, regards him, honors him, prefers him, venerates and esteems him. She defers to him, praises him, and loves and admires him exceedingly (1 Peter 3:1-2 Amp). In like manner, as a married woman, she is submissive to her own husband, subordinating herself as being secondary to and dependent on him and adapting herself to him, so that even if he does not obey the Word of God, he may be won over, not by discussion, but by her godly life, when he observes the pure and modest way in which she conducts herself, together with her reverence for her husband. That is, she feels for him all that reverence includes–respecting, deferring, revering him. Revering means to honor, esteem, appreciate, prize, and, in the human sense, adoring him; and adoring means to admire, praise, be devoted to, deeply love, and enjoy her husband.

She gets up before dawn to prepare breakfast for her household (Proverbs 31:15). Only the Lord can give understanding wives (Proverbs 19:14). She ministers the love chapter (1 Corinthians 13) to her family.

Her countenance then will change. A happy face means a glad heart; a sad face means a breaking heart (Proverbs 15:13). Her conversation will change (Proverbs 31:26). When she speaks, her words are wise, and kindness is the rule for everything she says. Everyone enjoys giving good advice, and how wonderful it is to be able to say the right thing at the right time (Proverbs 15:23)! For the Lord grants wisdom! His every word is a treasure of knowledge and understanding (Proverbs 2:6). Out of the abundance of her heart her mouth speaks (Matthew 12:34).

Because she realizes how much the Lord loves her, she will begin to love herself because of Christ within, and in turn love her neighbors as herself (Matthew 19:19).

Her relationship with Christ effects every facet of her home. She is thrifty, she is a hard worker and energetic. She can sew or buy nice clothing for her family. She is a woman of strength (of character) and dignity, and has no fear of old age. She watches carefully all that goes on throughout her household and is never lazy (Proverbs 31:13,17,18,21,25,27).

And because she puts the Lord first in her life (Matthew 6:33) her children stand and bless her; so does her husband. He praises her with these words: "There are many fine women in the world, but you are the best of them all!" (Proverbs 31:28-29)

Charm can be deceptive, and beauty doesn't last, but a woman who fears and reverences God shall be greatly praised. Praise her for the many fine things she does. These good deeds of hers shall bring her honor and recognition from even the leaders of the nation (Proverbs 31:30-31).

Note: These scriptures were taken from one of the following translations: *King James, Living,* or *Amplified.* Composed in 1976.

Notes

CHAPTER TEN

HARVESTING/REAPING

Sources: *Stocking Up III*, Carol Hupping, Rodale
Make It Last, Earl Proulx, Yankee Books
How To Do Just About Anything, Reader's Digest
Yankee Home Hints, Earl Proulx, Yankee Books

Harvesting Fruits and Vegetables. Making sure that you harvest your food at the right time is only half the key to great tasting fruits and vegetables kept through the winter months. Handling the food after the harvest–during the time between picking and processing–is just as important.

Although the actual growth of fruits and vegetables stops when they are plucked and cut off from their food supply, respiration and activity of enzymes continue. The physical and chemical qualities of the plants deteriorate rapidly. Not only will there be a degradation of appearance and flavor as the freshness of food fades, there will also be a loss of nutrients, particularly of the fragile vitamin C.

All should be prepared and canned as soon as possible after harvest. If you can, cool it right after you pick it. The best procedure is to immerse it in ice water; keep it between 32° and 40° or cover your product with cracked ice.

You can freeze, can, dry, pickle, or juice your produce.

Making flowers last *Fresh flowers* can be made to last longer if you pick them in the late afternoon. They have a greater sugar content then and will last longer than ones picked earlier in the day. Carry a bucket of warm water to the garden and immerse flower stems as soon as you cut them.

Cut flowers can be kept fresh longer if you put them in a vase containing a solution of 2 tablespoons of vinegar, 3 tablespoons of sugar and 1 quart of water. Use warm (not hot or cold) water (approx. 80° to 110° F is ideal).

Another preservative is to add equal parts of lemon-flavored soft drink to a vase of water. The additives lower the pH level, the sugar replaces glucose the plant has lost–and needs–and the carbonation keeps the bacterial growth in check.

Strip off all leaves which would otherwise end up under water. Avoid putting fresh cut flowers next to fruits and vegetables. The ethylene gas discharged by the vegetables can kill the flowers overnight. (This is another reason why you should not store bulbs in the refrigerator next to produce. The gases given off by the vegetables will cause the bulbs not to flower when planted.)

To dry flowers, cut them at, or just before, their peak of bloom. Choose only bright, perfect flowers and leaves for drying. Pick them just about noon on a clear, dry day, and make sure they are free of moisture, insects, and disease. Begin the drying procedures immediately. Be sure to leave the stems long. Remove the leaves and hang the flowers upside down in a dry, dark place for several weeks, or until they are dry.

Air drying is good for small flowers in clusters, such as yarrow, baby's breath, and hydrangea. Remove all leaves except ones near each blossom. Gather the flowers into small bunches and secure them with rubber bands. If you tie them with string or wire, tighten the ties every few days, as the stalks shrink as they dry. Hang them upside down in a dry, dark place for several weeks, or until they are dry.

Using a drying agent works best with flowers with thick heads, such as roses, zinnias, and daffodils. Use silica gel, available at craft stores, or perlite from a nursery or florist. The flowers are less likely to mildew and will retain their colors better. If the gel has absorbed moisture the crystals will be pink, so before you use it set it in a 250° oven for an hour or until it turns blue.

Spread a 1-inch layer of the drying agent in the bottom of an airtight container. Choose flowers of similar type and size, remove their leaves, and lop off all but ½ to 1 inch of stem.

On top of the agent, place cupped flowers (such as roses) upright, open faces face down, and sprays flat. Completely cover them with additional crystals. Seal and label the container and place it in a cool, dark place.

When the flower petals are almost as crisp as paper (in about a week), gently pour off the agent. Thread florist's wire through the flower heads and secure then with florist's tape to provide stems for arrangements.

For best results in *pressing*, pick flowers and leafy plants around noon. Orange and yellow blossoms retain their colors best, most blues and pinks fade, and reds turn brown. Lay each plant between two layers of absorbent paper (best for fleshy flowers) or waxed paper (fine for thin or delicate types). With thick heads, such as roses, press the petals individually. Weight the flowers with a heavy book or bricks, leave them in a warm, dry place for at least 4 weeks.

SPIRITUAL APPLICATION

My harvest is abundant when my seed is healthy and plentiful.

From *Daily Thoughts on Living Free* by Neva Coyle. "There are some citrus trees that have both fully ripe fruit on them and blossoms at the same time. It is like that with us. In some areas we may be mature and developed and in others areas just a little bud. It is a lifelong thing. I will always be producing a crop and promising a crop at the same time."

In Chapter 7 we spoke about pruning, and discussed John 15 where Jesus told us He is the true vine and His Father is the gardener. In verse 2 He states that a branch needs pruning to be more fruitful; to have a harvest. Psalm 1:3 states that we are (to be) like trees that grow beside a stream (thirsty for more of the Lord) bearing fruit at the right time (LB)–"they succeed in everything they do."

Our fruit is good works; our actions, attitudes and thoughts are those which glorify the Lord . There is an abundance of good in our hearts, and that is where our speech shows Who we are living for. Luke 6:45 states, "The mouth speaks what the heart is full of. A good person brings good things out of his treasure of good things; a bad person brings bad things out of his treasure of bad things."

Commentary in my *The Bible for Today's Christian Woman*, CEV addresses sharing our "harvest."

> "Realize God gives us plenty so we can share with others. One of God's promises to his people was the blessing of good crops. When Israel obeyed him, God sent rain and sunshine on the fields and protected the

wheat from destruction. Good harvests were a gift from God to those he loved.

"But the recipients of these blessings were not to keep all the grain for themselves. God gave them specific rules about harvesting. When farmers brought wheat in from the fields they were to leave plenty out there for the poor to pick up and eat. After all, orphans and widows didn't have fields. In the same way, growers of olives and grapes were to leave some fruit on the vines so those with no source of food could pick and eat them.

"Today, God still often chooses to meet the needs of the poor indirectly, instead of providing directly to those who are hungry, he may give extra to us, so we can take from our abundance and share with them.

"Has God blessed you with material things? Take the opportunity to give food, clothing, and other possessions to those who have less. (Deuteronomy 24:19)"

A practice of mine, which gives me great pleasure, is to "tithe" on things which are given to me: plants, produce, etc. I try to share some part with others. We have a practice in our church, also, scripturally motivated, of giving "first fruits" to our pastor. Some bring "first fruits" they harvest from their gardens. Others bring the "first fruit" of a raise they may have received. (Read over Deuteronomy 26 and Exodus 23:19.) These go to our pastor.

Is your life producing fruit only for yourself? Hosea 10:1 indicates Israel brought forth fruit for himself. A vine produces fruit for the gardener, not for itself. Selfishness can cause us to:

- Look out only for #1!
- Make ourselves an idol.
- Not put God first.
- Want to have the blessings of God but not the responsibilities, or to be known as children of God.

Our lives need to be fruitful for His glory.

Galatians 6:7-9 "—a man reaps what he sows. The one who sows to please his sinful nature, from that nature will reap destruction; the one who sows to please the Spirit, from the Spirit will reap eternal life. Let us not become weary in doing good, for at the proper time we will reap a harvest if we do not give up. Therefore, as we have opportunity, let us do good to all people, especially to those who belong to the family of believers."

Hayford's Bible Handbook has some excellent commentary on receiving a harvest:

> "(Luke 6:38). Jesus opened up a whole new way of giving, He gave Himself totally to and for the needs of the people. We can no longer pay or sacrifice our way into God's mercy. Jesus Christ has paid our debt before God, and His Cross is a completed work in our eternal interest. Our giving then, is no longer a debt that we owe, but a seed that we sow! The life and power source is from Him. Ours is simply to act on the power potential in that seed-life He has placed in us by His power and grace!

"Notice that when Jesus said, 'Give,' He also said, 'and it will be given to you.' Giving and receiving belong together. Only when we give are we in a position to expect to reach out and receive a harvest. And Jesus said the harvest will be 'good measure, pressed down, shaken together, and running over.'

"We give as to God, and we receive as from God; but we should remain sensitive at all times to the different ways in which God may deliver our harvest."

And then, "A due season for all seeds. (Galatians 6:7-9). God has a timetable for every seed we plant. His timetable is not always our timetable. Sometimes the 'due season' means a quick return. Sometimes it means a process or a slow return that may take a year–even a lifetime. But we can count on three things. First, God will cause a harvest to come from our seeds. Second, God is never early or late–He is always right on time with our best interests at heart. Third, our harvest will have the same nature as our seeds sown: good seeds bring good harvests, bad seeds bring bad harvests.

"What are we to do during the growing time of our seeds? (1) Refuse to become discouraged. (2) Determine to keep our faith alive and active. (3) Give and keep on giving; love and keep on loving. Know this–His harvest is guaranteed. Continue in an attitude of expectancy."

Some scriptures to meditate on:

Hebrews 12:11. "No discipline seems pleasant at the time, but painful. Later it produces a harvest of righteousness and peace for those who have been trained by it."

James 3:18. "Peacemakers who sow in peace raise a harvest of righteousness."

Romans 6:20-22. "When you were slaves to sin, you were free from the control of righteousness. What benefit did you reap at that time from the things you are now ashamed of? Those things result in death. But now that you have been set free from sin and have become slaves to God, the benefit you reap leads to holiness and the result is eternal life in Christ Jesus our Lord."

John 4:35. "Open your eyes and look at the fields. They are ripe for harvest."

Luke 10:2. The harvest is plentiful but workers are few. Ask the Lord of the harvest to send out workers to His harvest field."

Psalm 126:5-6. "Those who sow in tears will reap with songs of joy. He who goes out weeping, carrying seed to sow, will return with songs of joy, carrying sheaves with him."

Gary Stinnett is minister to students at Dotson Memorial Baptist Church. Not too long ago, Mr. Stinnett published an article in *The Daily Times*, titled, "It's up to us to spread the faith."

The article is too lengthy to add here, but in summary, he states, "Ninety-five percent of all Christians in North America will not win one person to Christ in their entire lifetime."

A quote from Donald McGavran, in the article, stated, "If top priority is not given to effective evangelism by our churches, in two generations the church in America will be much like its counterpart in Europe–practically nonexistent."

Mr. Stinnett went on to write, "It paints a pretty grim picture, doesn't it? As Christians, we were called to be 'fishers of men.' Unfortunately, as churches, it seems like instead of doing a lot of fishing, we're just keeping up the aquarium. Instead of finding ways to go out and catch new fish, we're content to swap fish that we've already caught, back and forth. 'Don't like your current aquarium? Well come try ours–we're algae free!'"

Then Mr. Stinnett lists five key principles to think about:

> "Presence - We have to establish a strong presence in the lives of those who need to hear about Christ. Do you realize that for the majority of those people who come to faith in Christ, the decisive factor is not a huge evangelistic rally or group event? It is the concern of a friend who takes the time to develop a one-on-one personal relationship with them.
>
> "We can't depend on preachers and ministers and evangelists and programs. We have to get out and meet people where they are and love them and win the right to share Christ with them.
>
> "Prayer - I've found that when I get real and earnestly pray and seek opportunities to share Christ with others, doors always seem to open." (Remember the prayer of Jabez that the Lord enlarge his territory?)
>
> "Proclamation - Just a fancy way of saying,

'communicating the message' of Christ. --- At some point in time, I'm convinced, we must be willing to speak up and tell people that without the forgiveness for their sins that comes upon accepting Jesus Christ as their Personal Savior, they are lost and hopeless.

"Persuasion - the ultimate goal is to persuade people to become followers of Christ. How? The quality of our lives. Could an unsaved person look at your life and see the unmistakable difference that Christ has made in it? Make a list of five things that being a Christian has done for you. Share these. Can others see them in your life on a daily basis? (My condensing.)

"Patience - most people make a profession of faith after a long conversion process, not as a result of a sudden meeting.

"- Jesus tells us 'Come to me - and I will give you rest.' But let me remind you, we can't spend all our time resting. The same Lord who said 'come' also told us to 'go' and share the Gospel with others. Jesus is still counting on you today to spread the message. How are you doing?"

God wants all His children employed in the harvest fields of the world. The Lord of Harvest has asked us to plant and harvest in our own neighborhoods; that we pick up the sheaves lying in our own communities. The employment is steady, and the wages are eternal in their reward.

Some notes I made at a conference about church growth state:

1. Don't lose them before they get started.
2. Make them feel welcome.
3. Get out of our comfort zones (where we always sit with our own circle) and get acquainted.
4. Put them in a comfortable place to sit during the church service.
5. Ask them to join you for breakfast (or lunch) if you go out; or invite them to your home to get acquainted. The important part is the fellowship.
6. Take their kids to Sunday School rooms, where applicable.
7. Get to know them.
8. Be friendly. Remember how you felt when you were new.
9. Find out their potential. Maybe they have a good voice or can play an instrument. Maybe they'd like to teach after they've been in your fellowship a while.

In thinking about this lesson, and ministering to people (the harvest) I wondered, "Do we clean them, peel them, know how to preserve them and store them? Are they under-ripe, ripe, or overripe? Are the birds stealing our fruit? Do we can them, freeze them, or dry them? Do we put them in a pressure cooker? What are our churches' capabilities for handling new people?

In another quote from *Hayford's Bible Handbook*, dealing with Isaiah 27:6 GNB "In the days to come, the people of Israel, the descendants of Jacob, will take root like a tree, and they will blossom and bud. The earth will be covered with the fruit they produce."

The same commentary further states, "The promise of restoration wipes away the earlier disappointment of an unfruitful vineyard. Now the Lord is planting anew, watering daily, clearing briars, and promising expansive fruitfulness. The picture is that of the Messiah, the true Vine (John 15:1-8) extending His disciples as fruit-bearing branches to the world. The fruit is the Lord's doing, yet He asks participants to come and be willing to be planted. Believers who are pliable before the Spirit–yielded to His direction and dynamic, willing to be stretched and sent forth—will bear much fruit."

FAMINE

I should not complete this chapter without warning about famine.

The Israelites became slaves because they were not prepared for famine. When their food ran out, they sold their livestock to buy food. When that supply was gone they sold themselves into slavery. (Read the story about famine and how the people were enslaved, starting in Genesis 41:25.)

In that context, do you realize we are selling ourselves into slavery to the banks when we live on credit cards? Proverbs 22:7 says, "The rich rule over the poor, and the borrower is servant to the lender."

Notes

CHAPTER ELEVEN

BIRDS, BEES, BUTTERFLIES AND CRITTERS

Source: *Attracting Birds to Your Backyard*, Sally Roth, Rodale Press, Inc.
North American Wildlife, Reader's Digest, 1982

Birds. Author Sally Roth says, "A yard without birds is like a half-finished picture. Plants and birds are just a natural combination. No matter how picture-perfect a garden may (or may not) be, it's the most enjoyable when it's filled with bird song as well as flowers.

"Spending time in a garden full of birds is the kind of therapy I like best. It calms my mind, erases the everyday woes and busyness of the workaday world for a few hours, and makes me remember what brings true happiness. A sprouting seed, a swelling bud, a new flower every morning; bluebirds in the nest box, a chickadee on my shoulder, the fluting of a wood thrush at dusk–nothing money can buy comes close to those treasures. Bringing the pleasures of plants and the lively antics of birds to your back yard will give you new surprises every day. A garden full of life is a garden full of love."

Something I'll bet you didn't know: a robin's bill is like tweezers, a woodpecker's like a chisel, a hummingbird's like a straw. Each one is especially "equipped" for the "work" they have to do to get food.

Birds are a flying SWAT team when it comes to insects. When you welcome birds into your garden, they'll thank you by eating hundreds of these pests each day–even more during their spring nesting season."

Insects	***Birds That Eat Them***
Ants	Flickers, wood thrushes, and other thrushes and swallows eat swarming ants on the wing.
Bees and wasps	Flycatchers, kingbirds, tanagers
Cicadas	House wrens, crows, cardinals
Cutworms	Bobwhites, robins, cuckoos, catbirds, brown thrashers
Flies, gnats, and midges	Flycatchers, swallows, martins, gnatcatchers
Grasshoppers, crickets, and locusts	Many insect-eating birds
Leafhoppers	Wrens, chickadees, warblers
Long-horned beetles	Woodpeckers
Mosquitoes	Almost all birds
Treehoppers	Flycatchers, blackbirds, vireos, kinglets

I think of birds as music in my garden. Just today, I watched a pileated woodpecker rat-a-tat-tat on a tree trunk. Then it "hollered" for quite a while at something I could not see. I'm so happy each spring when I start hearing the bobwhites calling. Then, at night, there's the whippoorwill. The song of the cardinal is beautiful. I'm learning to identify, by sound, many of the birds which come to our garden.

Birds are just as unique as humans: jays are domineering, and spunky. Mockingbirds are not afraid, robins and northern flickers are ground feeders, turkey buzzards and crows clear out carrion (road kill!). I think the more birds you have in your garden, the more beautiful it is, and the better it sounds.

Bees. Bees, as well as wasps and ants, have a social organization that is among the most elaborate in the animal world. Hundreds, even thousands, of individuals live in a communal nest, each with a task to perform. A queen lays eggs, and the short-lived males (or drones) do nothing but impregnate the queen. Workers gather, make, and store honey for the adults and the wormlike larvae.

Carpenter bees bore into wood around your home. If you find a hole from one, treat it with insecticide, fill the hole and paint over it. The paint will keep them from going back into the wood.

Honey bees will pollinate a fruit orchard and are desirable. A favorite honey in East Tennessee is the darker sourwood honey made from the flowers of the sourwood tree.

Bumblebees also are useful for pollinating. They pick up the pollen on the hairs of their legs and deposit it in the female part of the flower of fruits.

Butterflies. Like other insects, butterflies have three pairs of legs, but the front pair is usually reduced in size. Before they can fly, butterflies must warm their bodies to 81°, spreading their wings at various angles to catch the sun's rays, depending on what kind they are. They go through complete metamorphosis: egg, larva, pupa, and adult. They are "flying flowers", so beautiful in a garden. Planting the kind of vegetation they like will guarantee their presence. Some plants I have which are almost continually visited by butterflies, are Mexican sunflower and a pink chrysanthemum which is huge and covered with gorgeous daisy-like flowers, and of course, the butterfly bush.

Critters. The other day we met with the ranger in charge of the Kyker Bottoms Wildlife Preserve across the road from us. He was telling us that raccoons are getting to be a big problem by overpopulation. We, and our neighbors, could testify to that; we never got one of the ears of corn we were expecting from our garden last year.

Foxes are near also. One evening we had some chicken bones which needed to be put in the large trash receptacle, but my husband laid them on a bench outside our kitchen door, planning to deposit them in the bin the next morning.

Dan, our son, was working the night shift then, had come home, and was sitting on the front porch about 2:00 am. A fox came on to the porch (he had devoured the bones!) and walked within two feet of where Dan was sitting. Dan "spoke" to it, and it stopped in the front yard and just looked at him. Then it circled around to reenter the breezeway (where the bones had been) and stared at Dan for a long time. (He probably was wondering if any more food was going to appear.)

I mentioned earlier that birds make "music" in my garden. There's also the sound of water over rocks, wind in the trees, frogs croaking, June bugs and cicadas.

When we first moved on to our property, living in a 30' 5th wheel while our house was being built, I was so excited the first time I heard the bob whites and whippoorwills. Then one night, after we moved in to the house, a whippoorwill sat right under our open bedroom window and called and called. My goodness, was it ever loud! We finally had to turn on the outdoor light to get it to go away.

There's also the cry of a red-tailed hawk, honking of geese, quacking of ducks, and squawking of a lone pelican.

Southern Living magazine had an article in the January, 2003, issue with ideas and suggestions regarding birds in the winter garden. It stated:

"As temperatures dip, natural food supplies

dwindle, and birds must scratch the leaf-littered ground in search of seeds and insects to sustain them.

"Food for birds

Besides regular bird seeds, use suet cakes, dried fruit, peanuts, black oil sunflower seeds, fresh fruit, or shelled peanuts and mealy worms. To prevent green weed patches from the seeds, use a No-Mess blend which has little or no waste and won't sprout in your yard. Hang feeders at least 5 feet off the ground and 10 feet away from trees, shrubs, fences, or houses to keep squirrels at bay and eliminate ambush areas for cats.

"Water for Drinking and Bathing

It's critical to have flowing water. Mosquitoes can't reproduce in moving water, and babbling or splashing water sounds like a natural running creek, so the birds are drawn to it. Build shallow wading areas only 1 or 2 inches deep. They give birds a perfect place for bathing, which helps them clean their feathers of dirt and mites. Once the birds visit they remember the water source and return.

"Shelter and Nesting Sites

Birds need protection from the elements. Thick, bushy evergreen plants that block the wind and rain shield birds from cold or wet weather. Such cover also helps create escape routes to get away from predators.

> Shrubs with tight branching habits make good nesting sites. Birdhouses can also be placed around your home to provide secure spots for birds to raise their young. House wrens and doves will nest in hanging baskets filled with plants."

Smells in the garden can be honeysuckle, 4 o'clocks, roses, fresh rain, just-mown grass, dianthus, phlox, and on and on. How blessed we are to have noses!!

Our local newspaper ran an article by Beth Burwinkel of *Gennett News Service*, titled "Plants can keep deer from snacking." If deer are a problem for you, this may be helpful.

> "Each year, horticulture experts kept hearing the same request from homeowners tired of watching deer damage their gardens.
>
> "Gardeners want a list of plants that deer won't bother. When employees at the Cincinnati Zoo did some research, they couldn't find a good list of deer-resistant ornamental plants so they decided to make their own.
>
> "They compiled a survey form and distributed it to 400 people who would know about deer-resistant plants: nursery professionals, landscapers, extension agents, garden club members and experts from local arboretums and park districts.
>
> "Steve Foltz, director of horticulture at the zoo, is impressed with the detailed responses in the 60-plus replies he has received. While

he continues to study the answers, he is noticing early trends.

"**Question:** What are some plants that deer tend to not bother?
Answer: Deer are going to eat anything if they get hungry enough. But these plants appear to be deer-resistant: Russian sage, amsonia, shasta daisy, coreopsis, ferns, all ornamental grasses, helleborus, epimedium, lamiastrum, daffodils and brunnera. Good shrubs that deer tend to not bother are boxwood, butterfly bush, spiraea, and bayberry.

"**Question:** What plants are deer most likely to damage?
Answer: Hosta, phlox, sedum, daylilies, oakleaf hydrangea, Japanese yew, shrub roses, tulips, American arborvitae, burning bush, China boy holly and China girl holly.

"**Question:** What about annuals?
Answer: Sweet potato vine and impatiens are annuals that deer tend to eat. If you have a problem with deer in the garden, better annuals to plant include lantana, dusty miller, celosia, ageratum, salvia and creeping zinnia.

"**Question:** What are other options for controlling deer?
Answer: There are sprays on the market. Another option is an eight-foot tall mesh deer fence that you can string through

the trees in the woods. In the city, the best bet is probably to use plants that are the least favorite of deer and see what happens."

SPIRITUAL APPLICATION

The Lord visits my garden in many ways.

When we think of birds, bees, butterflies and critters, can you think of relationships with people in your life who may be one of these? Remember our lesson on companion planting?

Many of these "critters" can be fenced out. The enemy is always looking for some way to get in to our spiritual garden to take the fruit, or spoil it in some way. Fence him out with God's word. God's word hidden in our heart helps ward off the invasion of the enemy's "insects."

Song of Solomon 2:15 says the "little foxes" have spoiled the vineyard. The Bible dictionary defines foxes as cunning marauders. That's a thief. There are many "little foxes" in our lives which steal our peace: worry, anxiety, jealousy, and temptations of all kinds, to name a few.

Some scents draw insects; some colors. How are we attracting the enemy? Is there some spirit from our life before Christ which is still a "companion" and makes us more vulnerable?

There are some critters which come out only at night: insects, snakes, some animals. When we're walking in the "light" (1 John 1:7), "the blood of Jesus purifies us, and we have fellowship with one another."

All kinds of critters invade our lives: thoughts, suspicions, listening to the voice of the enemy, roots of bitterness, etc. There are critters which suck out our life: busyness, relationships which drain us, (there's companion planting again!).

Some chew away our blessings, faith and confidence in God: what we meditate on. Philippians 4:6-8 gives us a list of things to chew on which will build us up. We need to focus on God's promises, not the problems we see in our lives. Either God invades our spirit, or the enemy will. Our focus comes through our eyes or our ears to our spirit. Pray!!

Others bore into our spirits: anger, hopelessness, unforgiveness, bitterness. Hebrews 12:15 and Ephesians 4:31, Job 19:1 and 21:25 all speak of bitterness and its devastation in our lives.

Sin is the greatest invading critter. There are 20 references throughout the Bible which refer to the sin of Sodom and Gomorrah, found in Genesis 13. It's interesting to read about the area of Sodom. Genesis 13:10 says the plain of Jordan (where Sodom was located) was well watered, like the garden of the Lord, like the land of Egypt, toward Zoar. And Lot chose that area for his family to establish their home. But verse 13 says the men of Sodom were wicked and sinning greatly against the Lord. Genesis 19:12 and 13 tells that their sin was so great the Lord sent His angels to destroy the city, and He did. Lot's wife longed so much for what she had to leave behind (even though the Lord was rescuing them from all that sin) that the Lord destroyed her, too. Where she had lived (spiritually?) had deceived her and caused her destruction.

The Lord used plagues in the book of Exodus (chapters 7-11) to try to get Pharoah to release the Israelites: plagues on livestock, blood to water, flies, frogs, hail, locusts, boils, gnats, darkness, and on their firstborn. Livestock and frogs (Genesis 13:10) represented gods in Egypt: considered sacred. The Lord, through this plague, was attacking Egypt's god to show His power was far superior to all the supernatural powers of Egypt. (*Full Life Study Bible)*

Killing babies in the womb is a plague on this generation today.

What we see: Satan used the apple (in the garden of Eden) to invade the spirit of man. <u>He uses what we see</u>

to invade our spirit; like things we desire which are forbidden (pornography). The lust of things opens us to deception. The enemy then controls our spirit. That is what caused Eve to surrender to the deception.

Pride of life has to do with things: houses, possessions, bank accounts, social status, professional status, our own abilities and talents. 1 John 2:15-17 says, "Do not love the world or anything in the world. If anyone loves the world, the love of the Father is not in him. For everything in the world–the cravings of sinful man, the lust of his eyes, and the boasting of what he has and does–comes not from the Father but from the world. The world and its desires pass away, but the man who does the will of God lives forever."

What we imagine: Israel saw the inhabitants as giants and themselves as grasshoppers (Numbers 13:31-33). Israel was contemplating the conquest of the promised land. When they saw the giants they became fearful of what they saw. Fear and unbelief took over and cancelled their ability to have the promises of God. Joshua and Caleb had a firm commitment and full confidence in His promises. We see the pile of bills or a doctor's report and forget God's promises to provide for us (Matthew 6:25-34) and be our healer (Exodus 15:26, Psalm 103:3, Psalm 147:3).

There are many good things which come into our gardens, too. Some build nests and, like birds, stay a while. They are seasonal blessings: where you live for a time, where you go to church, relationships which are so dear, yet short-lived.

Debby Boone wrote in *Daily Devotions for Godly Women*, Zondervan: "I took out my journal to record some thoughts about this "nest" where I could lay down my own young. 1. A nest is a place of security, rest and provision. 2. It is a place to lay my children on God's altar daily. 3. It will take a sacrifice of time to seek knowledge and wisdom for my young. Psalm 84:3. 'Even the sparrow has found a home, and the swallow a nest for herself, where she may have her young'– a place near your altar, O Lord Almighty, my King and my God."

There are also beautiful, fleeting thoughts, like butterflies: the smile of a friend, a hug, an encouraging word, a kind deed, done for you or by you.

The power base of man's life is not the intellect. It is the spirit of man which is the power base of our life. Don't let Satan's "critters" invade your spiritual garden. Use God's Word to kill off those invaders.

Critters	**Fence to keep them out**
Disillusionment	John 16:33
Complaining	Jude 16, Philippians 2:14, Proverbs 15:13, 15, 17:22, Psalm 106:25
Expecting perfection	Romans 2:1-4, Romans 14-15:7, Ephesians 4:32
Your past	Philippians 3:12-17 (:17 companions)
Inconsistency	1 Timothy 4:15, 16
Lack of determination	Galatians 6:9, 1 Corinthians 15:58, 1 Peter 5:8,10
Temptations	1 Corinthians 10:13
Fear	2 Timothy 1:7
Habits (pornography, soaps, drugs, alcohol, overeating)	Philippians 4:13

According to James Hamilton, there are two kinds of Bible readers: those who skim the surface and those who dig deep. He describes them by comparing them to two common insects. He writes:

"One is remarkable for its imposing plumage, which shows in the sunbeams like the dust of gems; as you watch its jaunty gyrations over the fields and its minuet dance from flower to flower. You cannot help admiring its graceful activity, for it is plainly getting over a great deal of ground.

"But in the same field there is another worker whose brown vest and businesslike, straightforward flight may not have arrested your eye. His fluttering neighbor darts down here and there and sips elegantly wherever he can find a drop of ready nectar; but this dingy plodder makes a point of alighting everywhere, and wherever he alights he either finds honey or makes it. If the flower cup be deep, he goes down to the bottom. If its dragon-mouth be shut, he thrusts its lips asunder. And if the nectar be peculiar, he explores all about 'til he discovers it.

"His rival of the painted velvet wing has no patience for such dull and long-winded details.

"The one died last October. The other is warm in his hive, amidst the fragrant stores he has gathered."

Which type of Bible reader are you? Butterfly or bee?

<u>Bees and Buzzards</u>. *Quiet Times For Mothers*, Julia Graham, Access Publishing, 2001. (Note. I have changed the author's intent to be just for women, and made the message non-gender.)

> "Love is patient and kind...It does not become angry easily, and it does not remember wrong things that are done...It believes all things, hopes for all things and endures all things." (1 Corinthians 13:4-5,7)
>
> "Bees and buzzards are very different... buzzards circle above, looking for animals that are hurt or dead. Then they swoop down to tear on it. Honeybees are the exact opposite. They look only for the good sweet nectar, as they fly from flower to flower. Both buzzards and bees find what they're looking for–just as a spouse can usually find what they're looking for in their mate. They'll see what they want to see: the good–or the bad.
>
> "If we focus on our spouse's faults and mistakes, we'll find them. And the more fault we find, the less we'll respect them. When a spouse feels that their mate doesn't respect them...guess who's the last person they want to be with?
>
> "But if we try to look for the good qualities in our mates and focus on those, we can grow to respect and admire them. When they feel this respect from us, because we stop cutting them down and criticizing them, our marriages will be much happier. A wise person said, 'to your spouse's qualities and good points, be very kind, to their faults and

mistakes, a little blind.'

"A spouse needs to know that home is a safe place where they won't be criticized and put down the minute they walk in the door. If we could just guard and control our words and attitudes, think how peaceful our homes could be.

"There was a young married couple who really struggled to make enough money to live on. One day the husband took the little they had and bought a small service station. His wife didn't think this was a good investment–she knew he didn't have the time or knowledge to run the service station. The station soon went broke and they lost everything. The husband came home expecting his wife to be angry and to remind him that she'd told him not to do it. Instead she sat down with him and said, 'I've been doing some figuring. You don't smoke or drink alcohol, but if you had, we would have lost just as much money as we did with the service station. So don't worry, let's just forget it.'

"She could so easily have destroyed her husband's self-confidence that day. Instead she let him know she still believed in him. He went on to become a wonderful minister, known nationwide.

"There's a big difference between us and buzzards and bees. God made us so we can choose what we want to think, say, and do. But learning self-control and acceptance is much easier said than done. It's only with Christ's kind of love that we can do it! If we ask Him to help us, He'll fill our hearts with His love so we can give our spouses the respect and confidence they need from us." Tia Stanley

"Study your spouse as you would a rare plant. Minimize their faults and enlarge upon their virtues. After you have been talking upon their good qualities for some time, you will be surprised to find you believe what you say." Lilla Gertrude English, from *'Love Lights for Maid, Wife and Mother' (1912)*

Notes

CHAPTER TWELVE

SEASONS/WEATHER/LIGHT

The four seasons we enjoy are vividly obvious in East Tennessee. I am grateful for that. Each season represents a time of change. During spring, there is a great awakening in our gardens. Bulbs send out their vegetation and flowers. Perennials, bushes and trees begin to show life again. The air is still crisp; there's a sense of excitement because of the awakening of growth.

Then summer comes with increased sunshine and even more beauty and color in our gardens. The trees are full and provide shade. Birds are everywhere serenading us with their beautiful song. It's a time to be outside more, breathing in the wonderful clean air and feeling the warmth of the sun.

All too soon fall arrives. Color appears in different form; leaves turning. Then the leaves fall to the ground and soon the trees and bushes are bare. The temperatures are chilly, The garden is going to sleep.

During the dormant sleep of winter, plants and trees are still active through their roots, taking up water and nourishment. What we see appears to be dead, but it's only going through a season of quietness and rest. Temperatures are low and help the plants to stay still.

In not too long a time the slumbering ceases and spring is here again; a time of renewal.

In each season, light given by the sun and moon are different because of the earth's rotation and nearness to the equator. Plants vary in their need for light according to the amount of chlorophyl in their leaves. Some plants cannot exist in full sun; others cannot grow and develop without it. It is very important to know the light requirements of your plants so they can achieve their greatest potential. So it is, in the season, that the amount of light available will regulate the plant's "rhythms."

An excerpt from Cracker Barrel's 2004 Almanac is interesting. "Red Sky At Night, Sailor's Delight. Over the years, everyone from farmers to sailors has looked for ways to read the weather. While we can't always guarantee they'll work, here are some old adages we hope will keep you warm and dry.

Signs of good weather:

- A red sky in the evening means that the next day will be clear.
- A rainbow in the morning usually indicates clear skies for the rest of the day.
- Birds flying high in the sky means good weather will continue throughout the day.
- Wind blowing from the west is a sign of mild weather to come.

Signs of bad weather:

- A red sky in the morning is a sign of bad weather later that day.
- A rainbow in the evening predicts rain the following day.
- When the moon has a halo at night, it's a sign of rain or snow.
- Birds flying low in the sky is an indication of rain.
- When spiders repair their webs and make them bigger, it can be a sign of bad weather to come.
- Wind blowing from the east indicates harsh weather.
- If pigs gather leaves and hay, or flowers close their petals, a storm's brewing.

In March, 1998, *Horticulture* magazine had a very good article about weather, written by Eliot Tozer. It's lengthy, but very informative.

> "By watching the clouds and tracking the wind, gardeners are better able to predict the weather in their own back yards than are forecasters on television. As weather forecasters like to say, and most gardeners already know, all weather is local, really local.
>
> "Of course, all weather is also global. The earth's atmosphere is continuous and volatile, and a change in one place is followed by a change somewhere else. As the saying goes, 'When someone sneezes in Shanghai, it rains in San Francisco.'
>
> "The day-to-day variations in our atmosphere that we call weather can all be traced back to the sun, which heats our planet in a highly irregular manner. Equatorial regions receive more intense radiation than the poles, and land masses warm faster than the seas. The result is huge, homogeneous air masses, up to several thousand miles wide, that circulate around the planet, causing it to rain in one place and be sunny and dry in another. For example, when a mass of cold air trundles southeast from Canada and nudges under a mass of the lighter, warm air moving northeast from the Gulf of Mexico, precipitation usually results.
>
> "The rain or snow in this case will be heaviest

along the leading edge of the moving air mass, a boundary known as a front. If cold air is replacing warm air, we call it a cold front. If warm air is replacing cold air, it's a warm front. Warm fronts, too, are usually accompanied by unsettled weather and rain or snow.

"The good news is that the approach and passage of these fronts is marked by highly visible changes in the sky. The type of cloud, the direction of the wind, the temperature, and the atmospheric pressure all change, and these changes can be easily noted. If you watch the clouds and track the wind–and, for a sharper image, record the change in temperature and atmospheric pressure–you can reliably predict what the weather will be in your vicinity for at least the next couple of days.

"Mare's tails and a mackerel sky
Never leave the ground dry.

"Folk wisdom such as this, and there is a lot of it, can help you gauge the future. The 'mackerel sky,' in this case, is a type of altocumulus cloud–putty, midlevel clouds with a ripplelike pattern that resembles the scales of a fish. Generally moving from west to east, this cloud cover usually signals the arrival of a cold front within the next day. The actual arrival of the cold front is accompanied by cumulonimbi-towering thunderheads that produce lightning and rain (or snow). As the cold front passes, the earth below is deluged with short, heavy showers. The wind shifts from southwest to northwest and may blow for a day or two (what are known as 'blue northers' in Texas), the temperature falls, and the atmospheric pressure rises. High pressure weather is usually clear, cooler, and dry. Again, folklore has a couplet for it.

"When swallows fly high
We'll have clear, blue sky.

"Clear skies are full of high flying insects on which the birds feed. When foul weather threatens, the insects take cover. Or more poetically:

"When swallows fly low,
We'll have a blow.

"You can check the atmospheric pressure with a barometer, but the flight of birds can give you some indication of whether the glass is high or low.

"While a mackerel sky often signals the arrival of a cold front, the arrival of a warm front is presaged by cirrus clouds–wispy, featherlike, high level clouds called 'mare's tails.' Behind the cirrus mare's tails come altostratus, or sheet clouds–low level clouds that thickly cover the entire sky and veil the sun so that it seems to be shining weakly through ground glass. Nimbostratus clouds follow next, bringing with them a gray day.

Rain tends to be widespread, coming steadily or in long showers alternating with drizzle. Behind the front, the wind shifts from southeast to southwest, the temperature rises, and the pressure falls. Winds are steady and gentle.

"When a cow scratches her ear,
Rain is near.

"Whether the sign is birds flying low, insects landing on cattle, or a falling barometer, dropping air pressure is the sign of an approaching low pressure system, or low, as it is called, and accompanying bad weather. Such low pressure systems march across the United States every five or six days, summer and winter, a steady procession of waves in the boundary between warm air to the south and cold air to the north. Lows are made up of two fronts. On your weather map, this wave looks like an inverted V, with the right-hand leg a warm front and the left-hand leg a cold front. The system may be hundreds of miles across. It takes three to five days for this system to pass a given point, with characteristic changes in cloud type, wind direction, temperature, and atmospheric pressure.

"If the center of the low, the point of the inverted V, passes north of you, you will see cirri first. Then, stratus clouds will lower and thicken. In about 24 hours, depending on how fast the system is moving, the warm front passes first and precipitation begins. The wind changes from southeast to southwest and the temperature rises.

"A wind from the south has rain in her mouth.

"Another sign of the approaching warm front is a halo around the sun or moon. It is caused when light shines through tiny ice crystals at high altitudes.

"Halo around the sun or moon,
Rain or snow comes very soon.

"After the warm front passes, you enter the 'dry tongue,' with warm, pleasant weather. Cumulus humilis–fair-weather, low-level clouds with flat bottoms-dot the skies, and the wind becomes southwesterly. But within a day or two, the trailing cold front approaches, bearing sudden, heavy showers. The wind shifts from southwest to northwest and cooler, dry air settles in.

"The precipitation in a low often forms in bands, producing showers that last no more than a few hours. Hence the saying,

"Rain before seven,
Clear before eleven.

"But if the center of the low passes south of you, the sky is first painted with mare's tails before quickly becoming overcast with a low-level layer of rain clouds, or nimbostrati. Rain can fall steadily for three or four days. The wind shifts from northeast to northwest–'backing,' the meteorologists call it–and the air stays cool and damp, creating raw days.

"Lows follow a handful of tracks: due eastward from the Pacific Ocean, southeast from Canada, and northeast from the Gulf of Mexico. The East Coast of the United States gets its heaviest weather when a low from the Gulf runs 'outside' up the Atlantic coast, maintaining its strength by drawing moisture from the ocean.

"Lakes and ponds also affect precipitation. Locations on the downwind, or leeward side of a body of water usually get more precipitation than the upwind, or windward, side as the result of the air picking up moisture as it crosses the body of water. This additional snow or rain is termed a 'lake effect.'

"The same is true of mountains. Air flowing up the windward side cools down, and its moisture condenses out as rain or snow. Thus, the windward side of mountain ranges tends to be wet. Land on the leeward side, on the other hand, is often in a 'rain shadow' because air flowing downhill compresses, warms up, and dries out.

"Gardeners aren't just concerned about whether it is going to rain. Equally important is the subject of frost. And here, it's location that makes the most difference. Cold air, being heavier than warm air, sinks. The lower in elevation a garden is, the more likely it is to get frost. A difference of a couple of hundred feet can mean a difference of a month or more in the growing season. Because bodies of water change temperature more slowly than land, a garden next to a lake or pond will also get a few additional frost-free days.

"All other things being equal, if the temperature is 50 degrees or lower at sunset, the sky is clear and there's no wind, frost can be expected overnight. With no blanket of clouds to keep the earth's heat in, the earth radiates heat back to space and the temperature drops. Also, if there's no wind, the layer of cold air produced by the heat loss hovers at ground level instead of mixing with the warmer air above.

"If your soil is wet, there will be more moisture in the air to evaporate, and because heat is released when water evaporates, the air temperature near the ground will rise.

"If your garden is surrounded by trees, frost is less likely; the trees act as a blanket, keeping radiated heat in. Larger clearings, however, can increase the chance of frost as the surrounding trees create a low pocket into which cold air settles.

"Mulched plants will frost earlier than those

growing in bare soil because bare soil will more freely radiate heat at night, keeping the air around the plants warmer.

"Finally, if the wind is out of the southeast, temperatures will be higher; out of the west, lower.

"All of these rules, however, have exceptions. Weather forecasting, whether done by professionals or amateurs, is a notoriously inexact science. The one thing that is absolutely certain about weather predicting is that you'll be wrong a certain percentage of the time."

The *Mini Page* in our local newspaper had an article titled "Pretty, Powerful Clouds," which in very simple terms teaches about clouds.

"**What is a cloud?** A cloud is a clump of tiny water droplets or ice crystals floating in the atmosphere. The atmosphere is an envelope of gases (such as oxygen) that surrounds the Earth. Water vapor, which is water in gas form, is also in the atmosphere.

"How clouds form. When water vapor rises in the atmosphere, it grows colder, which causes the water vapor to turn into liquid water. Or if it is really cold, the vapor turns into ice crystals. The drops of water and ice crystals come together to make cloud droplets. When water is in the form of gas, it is invisible. But when it turns to liquid or ice, we can see it. We see clouds.

"Cloud colors. When we look up, clouds usually look white. But if they are filled with a lot of water, they block out so much sunlight that they look gray. Because thunderclouds are filled with rain and ice, they look very dark and gray.

"If you look up and see clouds with a greenish color, it means there is hail in those clouds. When clouds look green, they are especially dangerous. Strong storms including tornados can come out of this type of cloud. If you see green colored clouds, go inside at once.

"Clouds bring moisture to Earth. After clouds form, what happens next is either:

1. The water droplets evaporate, or turn back into gas.
2. Or water droplets come together. When enough join together, they form a raindrop or snowflake. When the raindrops or snowflakes grow big enough, they fall to Earth.

"Clouds change temperatures. At night during winter, clouds can act as a blanket over the Earth, keeping some of the sun's warmth from escaping back into space. Cloudy winter nights may be as much as 15 degrees warmer than nights that are clear. But during the day, clouds block some of the sun's rays from reaching Earth. Cloudy days can be cooler days.

"Types of Clouds.

1. Cirrus (SEER-us) are the highest clouds, floating from 16,000 to 45,000 feet up in the air.
2. Stratus (STRAT-us) clouds float from about 6,500 to 23,000 feet high. When stratus clouds are overhead, the whole sky looks gray. Steady rains and snowfalls fall from this type of cloud.
3. Cumulus (KYOOM-you-lus) are the lowest clouds floating from the surface of the Earth to about 6,500 feet high. They don't always fill the whole sky, which can cause some weird events. For example: Have you ever been on one side of the street with a blue sky overhead and no rain falling on you? But right across the street, the sky was dark with cumulus clouds, and rain was pouring down.

"Fog, a different type of cloud. Fog is a cloud that forms on the ground. When you are out on a foggy day, you are standing inside a cloud.

"Thunderheads. Scientists divide the main cloud types into groups. They add different word forms to the beginning or ending of cloud names to tell more about the cloud type. For example, when 'nimbus' is added to the end of a cloud name, it means the cloud is forming precipitation. Cumulus +nimbus together form 'cumulonimbus,' which are thunder clouds.

“**Storm safety.** Stay alert to changing weather conditions. When the sky turns very black, dark gray or green, and when the wind picks up, a storm is approaching. Do NOT stay outside.

“Use a National Oceanic & Atmospheric Administration (NOAA) weather radio. These radios will sound an alert tone if dangerous weather is coming to your area, even if the radio is not turned on. Any time you hear thunder or see lightning, even in the distance, go inside at once. Go inside a building or vehicle. If there is a tornado warning, do not stay in your vehicle. The best place to be is in a basement or interior room, such as a closet or bathroom, away from outside walls and windows.”

The following four pages give some guidance for working in your garden during each of the four seasons.

FOUR-SEASON YARD AND GARDEN CALENDAR

SPRING

If you get started early, you can have a truly beautiful yard by summer.

GENERAL

- Inspect your yard and garden to see what damage winter may have wrought. Plan for the new season. Visit your local nursery early and often.
- Rerake flower beds, prune dead limbs and replant whatever plants may have been pushed to the surface during cold weather.
- Begin to water ground covers as soon as weather permits.
- Weed and mulch flower beds and replenish them with new organic matter.

PERENNIALS

- Divide summer perennials for transplanting.
- Cut away any dead material and remove winter mulch from perennial beds.
- Apply plant food as soon as there is any sign of growth.
- Pay attention to where things are growing, so you can begin planting to fill gaps.
- Plant summer-flowering bulbs in late spring.
- Don't count on seeds if you are starting your first perennial garden. Few if any plants you start from seed now will flower this summer. Buy flats of year-old plants from the nursery.

ANNUALS

- Plant hardy annuals like phlox, snapdragon, calendula and clarkia outdoors as soon as the soil is workable.
- Using starter trays, pot other annuals indoors. In late spring move them outdoors.

LAWN

- Plant grass seed or plugs early in spring to ensure full growth by warm weather. Sod can be laid in late spring.
- Aerate and fertilize existing lawn areas.
- This is a good time to re-establish the boundaries between flower beds and lawn.

TREES AND SHRUBS

- Trim dead and damaged tree and shrub limbs.
- Many varieties of shrubs need to be trimmed back in the spring to stimulate new growth.
- Fertilize and mulch.

VINES AND CLIMBERS

- Tie off climbing vines.
- Cut back hybrid climbing roses to 6 inches for a few large blooms or to 12 inches if you want more of the smaller blooms.

98 HOME REMODELING

SUMMER

Once you've gotten things going, staying on top of your yard and garden maintenance means more time for enjoyment.

GENERAL

- As the weather warms, pay close attention to the watering needs of all your plants. They get thirsty quickly, and under-watering can cause damage.
- Use soaker hoses for beds. They will get the water right to the roots where it's needed.
- If you water with a sprinkler, water in the morning, when it is still cool. At high noon, water from sprinklers will evaporate too quickly, and in the evening, it will turn your plants soggy.
- If you vacation in the summer, remember to arrange for a neighbor to water occasionally. Better yet, you can buy timers that will do the job.

PERENNIALS

- Tall, spiky perennial flowers, such as delphiniums, foxglove, irises, gayfeather, acanthus and lupines, will need staking as they reach full height. Do this sooner rather than later, since stems can break under the weight of the plants when full grown.
- To encourage branching and create a more densely flowering plant, constantly "pinch off," or prune the plant.
- As flowers bloom and fade through the season, remove those flowers that have remained past their peak. This will help direct the plants' energies into new growth.
- You can continue planting late-blooming perennials and even bulbs until early July in most areas of the country. Use these to fill in weak spots in your garden throughout the early part of the summer.

ANNUALS

- Weed early and often.
- Check regularly for pests and blights. Annuals are particularly susceptible, so catching problems early and treating them will make life easier for you and your plants.
- Annuals may be planted throughout the season to maintain a fully blooming garden.
- As with all flowering plants, annuals should have dead blooms quickly removed.

LAWN

- Dethatch and aerate your lawn at regular intervals.
- Apply weed-killers and fertilizer early and then on a regular basis.
- Weed constantly.

TREES AND SHRUBS

- Maintain mulch around shrubs all summer. For evergreens and other acid-loving shrubs like rhododendrons and azaleas, use an acidic mulch like pine bark.

VINES AND CLIMBERS

- Climbing roses need to have faded blooms continuously deadheaded (i.e., removed).
- Be vigilant against pests and diseases.

ILLUSTRATIONS: DAVID STILES

FALL

This is the season for cleaning up, taking stock of your efforts and preparing your plants for cold weather.

GENERAL

- Rake, shred and compost fallen leaves.
- Keep watering and fertilizing your plants and lawn until the temperature reaches freezing.
- Gather flowers and herbs suitable for drying.

PERENNIALS

- Clear beds of all dead plant material to minimize risk of disease.
- Dig up perennial plants and bulbs that are not winter hardy and those that need to be divided before next spring.
- Plant spring-flowering bulbs like tulips, daffodils and hyacinths.
- Apply a generous layer of winter mulch to perennial beds to protect those plants that will be in the ground through the winter. The freeze-thaw cycle of winter weather can push some young plants to the surface, and if they are not protected by mulch, they will be killed.

ANNUALS

- Prepare flower beds for next spring by adding fertilizer and organic matter while turning and tilling soil.

LAWN

- Autumn is a good time to seed new lawns or bare spots in old lawns.
- Continue mowing, feeding and watering the lawn, although less frequently, right into the beginning of winter.

TREES AND SHRUBS

- Early autumn is a good time to plant new trees.
- Water trees and shrubs generously as they go dormant.
- Support young trees with stakes and guy wires.
- Protect any small shrubs beneath the house eaves that may be damaged by falling snow and ice.
- Wrap fruit trees to prevent damage by mice.

VINES AND CLIMBERS

- Autumn, when climbing vines become dormant, is a good time to install a trellis or latticework, instead of in the spring, when you have much else to do and run the risk of having fast-growing vines get ahead of you.

WINTER

Keep an eye out for cold-weather damage and plan for a bigger, better garden next summer.

GENERAL

- If your winters are warm and dry, continue watering outdoor plants through the season, whenever the temperature is above freezing.
- Begin planning next summer's garden. Learn from the mistakes of the past season and build on the strengths. A common mistake for beginners is to have their flower blooms all happen in only one stretch of the season. Another is to have the size and color of their flowering plants out of balance. Planning now will help remedy those problems. Better yet, draw a planting plan to guide you through the season.
- Once you have figured out what you are planting, and when and where you are planting it, order bulbs, seeds and shrubs early.

PERENNIALS

- Inspect perennial beds throughout the winter to make sure the plants you have left in the ground are surviving. Replenish any winter mulch that winter's winds may blow away.
- Shop for bulbs and seeds for the following season.
- Use starter trays to get a new crop of perennials going.

ANNUALS

- As winter winds down you can start to plant seeds in starter trays. Use a high-draining, richly organic potting medium. Find a sunny window and then water diligently.

LAWN

- Apply winterizing fertilizer and lime to your lawn. Lime keeps down the acidity of the soil, which is good for the grass. You can also use ashes from your fireplace or wood stove. Ashes are a good source of low-acidity potassium.

TREES AND SHRUBS

- Remove any ice and snow from evergreens after each storm.
- Winter is a good time to prune dormant trees. Do this during periods of thaw.
- You can also begin to force branches of spring-flowering shrubs.

VINES AND CLIMBERS

- Keep an eye out for ice damage to vines.
- Regularly check and secure ties on established vines.
- In warmer regions, late winter is the time to plant some varieties of climbing roses.

"Why do trees take their clothes off when it starts getting cold?"

Everyone has special days that define the year. For those who rarely stick their nose beyond their door, those days may be birthdays, holidays, or vacations. But for those of us who value our time outdoors, the year is a series of notable events, strung together in a messy, jumbled, absolutely delightful train that starts in the depths of winter and gathers speed through spring, summer, and autumn.

In fact, learning the sequence of the natural year is one of the greatest joys I know. It isn't merely a question of knowing, for instance, when the raspberries in my neighbor's fencerow will be ripe, so I can beat the catbirds and thrashers to a few handfuls. Knowing the rhythm of the land is essential if you're to have a deeper connection to it.

That timing differs from place to place, of course; when my corner of Pennsylvania is luxuriating in spring flowers and early honeybees, my friends in Vermont are likely to still be shoveling snow. Spring comes to the valleys earlier than the hilltops, while the mountains will show fall color weeks before the lowlands.

But the pace is remarkably consistent, even across huge areas of countryside. Many natural events—the timing of bird migration, the flowering of plants—are tied closely to average temperature, and the same agricultural zone maps gardeners use can provide a rough guide to when you can expect just what. I'm in the mountains of eastern Pennsylvania, in USDA Zone 6. The spring wildflower bloom here, for example, is about a week and a half behind Zone 7 in Delaware, Maryland, and central Virginia, and about the same length of time ahead of Zone 5, which splashes across the northern plateau of Pennsylvania and parts of New York and southern New England.

The pages that follow are a look at the year ahead, including dozens of those banner days—when the white-tailed fawns appear, when the garden gives up its first strawberries, when to expect the woolly bear caterpillars in autumn. Those dates are based on my records here at home, so add or subtract time depending on your own location.

I've been noting the seasonal comings and goings around my house for years, jotting them down in an old desk calendar with a notation of the year. At a glance I can see, for example, when the hummingbirds usually arrive in spring, so I can have their feeders filled and waiting for them.

Ultimately, these observations and dates are meant more for inspiration than guidance; if you live in the Plains, or the Southwest, or along the Pacific coast, the players will be much different. But events happen in every corner of the continent, and even the smallest back yard is brimming with seasonal miracles—if only we take the time to notice them.

JANUARY

January is marked by absences: of warmth, of light, of movement. December has the solstice and the shortest day, but January seems the darker month, when the sun hurries to the horizon, abdicating the world to snow and ice. The woods stand silent, and even the chickadees can do little to lighten the mood.

But however minimal January's pulse may seem, it never ceases completely. I remember a late afternoon when the clouds were heavy and the twilight came even earlier than usual. In advance of a storm the air was completely calm, and I was far back in the woods on my skis, trying to beat the snow home. The world was white, gray, and black, as still as a painting—but then my eye caught the subtlest of movements. A deer, standing as motionless as the hemlocks, was exhaling a tendril of steam that snaked in air currents I could not feel. Suddenly, the January woods seemed not half so frozen and empty as they had before.

Journal Notes

2 Great horned owls courting early this month; the male's voice is deeper, even though he is smaller than his mate.

5 Black bears giving birth in dens first several weeks of this month.

9 Watch for northern wanderers—evening grosbeaks, purple finches, common redpolls, and other migrant finches.

13 On cold nights, many songbirds (such as titmice, chickadees, and bluebirds) use empty nest boxes as roost sites. You can erect true roost boxes for them, with entrance holes at the bottom and a series of perches inside.

18 Red foxes—solitary for much of the year—pairing up for mating season. Listen for pairs yipping and squalling at night, and check fields and woods for twinned sets of tracks.

31 First turkey vultures arrive—spring's earliest migrants.

Surviving the Cold

Here in the Northeast, the winter of 1993-94 was one of the worst in memory, with deep, long-lasting snow and extreme cold that lingered for weeks. Many people openly worried about massive wildlife deaths.

The winter did kill some animals, of course, but by and large the deer, turkeys, songbirds, and others came through in fine shape. Wild animals have been dealing with harsh weather for millennia, and they're pretty good at it. Deer, for instance, conserve energy by moving as little as possible and staying close to good browse such as red maple saplings. Chickadees and other songbirds may even drop into a torpor at night, lowering their body temperature to save valuable calories.

Sky Watch

New moon: January 1
Quadrantid meteor shower: January 3
First quarter: January 8
Full moon: January 16
Last quarter: January 24
New moon: January 30

The luckiest may be the hibernators, such as bats, jumping mice, and woodchucks, which simply sleep the season away. Other mammals that den up for the winter—chipmunks are a good example—may have to awaken periodically to feed from their underground food caches. Bears, which do not feed through the winter, drop into a prolonged slumber that isn't quite true hibernation. Female bears even give birth while in their dens. When they emerge in early spring, their tiny newborns will have become active, wide-eyed, 10-pound cubs.

FEBRUARY

Short though it may be, February manages to fit a lot of slop into its 28 days—snow, ice, sleet, rain, mud, and more. But, often as not, February offers the first taste of spring as well, with a thaw or two just to remind you of what's waiting in the wings.

From inside the house, there's little to distinguish February from the frigid weeks that preceded it. Take a walk on a sunny day, though, and you get a sense of anticipation—subtle, but definitely there. The sun is a little higher in the sky than it was last month, and it shines a few minutes longer with each passing week.

The wild animals recognize the significance of those lengthening days. The tufted titmice begin their courtship songs this month, lilting strings of *peter-peter-peter;* the downy woodpeckers drum maniacally on hollow branches, their way of accomplishing the same thing. At the feeder, the male juncos may square off, chest to chest, or sing their machine-gun trills from the top of bare maples. They know it, even if we don't: Spring is coming.

Great Horned Owls

I know of no tougher, more adaptable bird than the great horned owl. This most powerful (though not the largest) of North American owls is found in almost every corner of the Western Hemisphere, from the Arctic tree line to the Amazon and Tierra del Fuego. Closer to home, the great horned's hoots echo not only through wilderness forests, but also in farm woodlots, shady suburban streets, and city parks. I once saw an owl flying waist high down a deserted city street late at night, obviously on the hunt.

In my area, great horned owls are the earliest of all birds to breed. Their courtship begins in late December, although for many pairs it is a matter of strengthening old bonds rather than finding a new mate. The female selects a nest site in January or early February, usually picking an old crow or hawk nest. A biologist I know once found an owl incubating her eggs in a used blue jay nest so small it all but vanished under her bulk.

The eggs will hatch in March, having been sheltered tirelessly from cold, snow, and sleet. The chicks need about two months to fully develop, but many leave the nest in early April, weeks before they can fly, scrambling through the branches, or jumping to the ground far below. The adults, looking like harried commuters, make the rounds among their scattered offspring, delivering food and warding off danger.

Sky Watch

First quarter: February 7
Full moon: February 15
Last quarter: February 22

Journal Notes

2 Fur on muskrats, beavers, and other aquatic mammals is at its thickest this month—"prime," as trappers say—providing best insulation for them.

5 On mild days, watch for mourning cloak butterflies, which are active in winter. Their dark purplish-black wings, edged with yellow, easily absorb the weak winter sun's warmth.

9 Skunk cabbage opening in wetlands—the first wildflower of spring. The flower's rotten-meat odor attracts flies, which are active earlier than bees.

11 Great horned owls laying one to four eggs, brooding constantly to protect against cold.

15 Watch feeders for brown house finches that sing on mild days—they are immature males.

19 Northern flying squirrels mating; litters will be born in late March or early April.

21 Male goldfinches begin to turn yellow as olive tips of body feathers wear off, revealing gold underneath. Process will continue until males are bright yellow in spring.

25 Drive carefully at night—amorous cottontails, skunks, and opossums are abroad in large numbers.

28 Male red-winged blackbirds arrive in marshes; females will follow in a week or two, after territories are established.

MARCH

Never turn your back on March. It will lull you into a false sense of security with a string of mild days, then smack you behind the ear with a snowstorm that buries the daffodils right up to their buds.

For all that, I love March. Around here, it is the month when things start moving—when the land shrugs off its load of snow and starts to act alive. If the month is mild, the spring peepers and wood frogs will begin to clamor in the marshes by mid-March, and the waterfowl will pour north in the wake of the thawing ice.

Best of all, there usually comes one day early in the month, when the wind is warm and blowing hard from the south, that the sky fills with Canada geese. These aren't the low-flying local birds that have been around all winter, hopping from cornfield to frozen pond and back again; these geese are strung out against the blue in ragged lines and chevrons so high you can barely see them against the clouds. But always you can hear them, a wild gabble that runs through me like an electric shock, and tells me spring has won the battle again.

Journal Notes

1 If mild, expect first robin flocks about now. Time to clean out bluebird boxes.

5 Cardinals, song sparrows, and house finches singing.

9 Peak of northbound tundra swan migration. If ice is gone, red-spotted newts courting in ponds.

11 Great horned owl eggs begin hatching, producing the first baby birds of the year.

13 Spotted salamanders migrate to breeding ponds on first mild, rainy night.

15 Ring-necked pheasants cackling in the fencerows. Painted turtles sunning on logs and rocks on mild days.

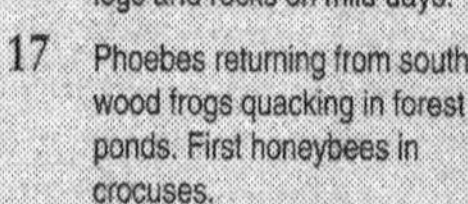

17 Phoebes returning from south; wood frogs quacking in forest ponds. First honeybees in crocuses.

19 Spring peepers join amphibian chorus; woodcocks performing sky dances at dusk. Red-tailed hawks sitting on eggs.

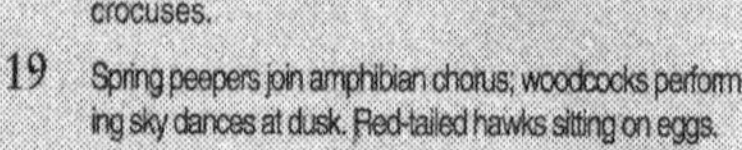

23 Red maples and quaking aspens blooming. Early rabbit nests in flower beds and meadows. Pregnant woodchucks carrying fresh nesting material down holes.

25 Field sparrows singing; doves building nests.

30 Tree swallows return; a few bluebirds sitting on eggs. American toads singing in marshes.

The Sky Dance Of the Woodcock

A woodcock is an unlikely aerialist. Dumpy as a couch potato, with bugged eyes and a long, knitting-needle beak, this unusual shorebird spends most of its time in damp woods and meadows probing for earthworms. But with early spring the males show an unexpected grace in the air.

Sky Watch

New moon: March 1
First quarter: March 9
Full moon: March 17
Vernal (spring) equinox: March 21
Last quarter: March 23
New moon: March 31

Each March evening at dusk, the male woodcocks gather at traditional *leks*, or courtship sites, usually a somewhat overgrown field near a stream or wet forest. Here they puff up, then give an explosive, nasal *peent!* that sounds more like a frog or a machine than a bird. The call comes every few seconds for several minutes; then a male woodcock will launch himself into the air, spiraling upward on twittering wings (the twittering sound comes from modified wing feathers that whistle in the wind).

You can just barely see him against the western sky when he reaches his peak. Then, unexpectedly, he begins to fall out of control. The whistle of the wings is replaced by a gurgle. A second or two before he splats against the ground, the woodcock rights himself, lands—and starts the whole improbable performance again.

APRIL

April cannot make up its mind—winter one minute, spring the next, sometimes a dash of summer in the mix to keep you guessing. Mostly, though, April is promise, the month when change comes fastest to the fields and woods.

The first flush of wildflowers bloom in the woods, shining in sunlight that will disappear in a few weeks behind the tree leaves. Trout lilies, with mottled leaves that look like a brook trout's back, grow beside the streams where the fish themselves live—a situation I have always felt exceeds coincidence. In the back yard, violets and dandelions bloom together, blue and yellow, a combination too pretty to be labeled weedy.

Especially in April's second half, the spring bird migration quickly builds steam. Swallows and summer sparrows return, along with the first warblers and early vireos. But my April is complete when the wood thrushes come back, filling the dawn with their liquid songs. It makes me think of Thoreau's description: "Whenever a man hears it he is young, and Nature is in her spring."

Wet Singers of Spring

Not all the songs of spring come from birds in the trees. On gentle April nights the marshes and ponds ring with songs that are just as sweet—and a *lot* louder—than the bird chorus at dawn.

The singers are frogs and toads, which crowd into wetlands in early spring to breed. In my neck of the woods the concert begins with the wood frogs in mid- to late-March (depending on how mild the spring has been). Wood frogs, brown with black raccoonlike masks, jumble together in shallow woodland pools, quacking like ducks—in fact, most people who hear the racket don't realize they're listening to frogs.

A week or two later the most famous of the amphibian singers begin to call. Spring peepers may be only an inch or so long, but their voices carry for a mile or more on a still night, and standing in a marsh surrounded by hundreds of them is deafening. The males inflate their balloonlike vocal sac and belt out a high, ascending *preeep!* If another male comes too close, you'll hear a staccato version that means "Back off."

The wood frogs end quickly, but the peepers continue to sing through April and May, joined by American toads (which have a lovely, buzzing trill), green frogs (which plunk like out-of-tune banjo strings) and pickerel frogs (which snore). All you need to enjoy the concert is a pair of boots, a flashlight, and a dash of adventure.

Sky Watch

First quarter: April 8
Full moon: April 15
Lyrid meteor shower: April 21
Last quarter: April 22
New moon: April 29

Journal Notes

1 Gray squirrels giving birth in tree cavities.

3 Bloodroot blooming in woods; first cabbage white and spring azure butterflies. Turkey gobblers sounding off at dawn each day.

7 White, frothy flowers of shadbush (also known as shadberry, shadblow, or serviceberry) brighten fencerows. Northbound ospreys fishing in ponds and rivers.

11 First barn swallows and chipping sparrows appear. Woodchucks giving birth.

15 Broad-winged hawks returning from tropics. First palm and pine warblers moving through.

20 Blue jays nesting, catbirds and blue-gray gnatcatchers migrating through. Trailing arbutus and hepatica blooming.

26 Wood thrush, veery, and hermit thrush arrive. Wood turtles and box turtles active. Most robin eggs laid and incubation begun.

30 March marigolds and black cherries in full bloom. Snapping turtles laying eggs in sandy, sunny areas near water.

MAY

If April is the promise, with its fickle weather and hint of color, then May is the payoff. This month spring cascades across the landscape in her full glory, with new leaves unfurling in vivid green, wildflowers carpeting fields, and birds and insects rushing to return.

Each May the world is awash in babies. The robins that spent late April building nests, gleaning the dried grass from my meadow and mud from my marsh for the construction, now are producing a bumper crop of chicks. So, too, are the bluebirds and tree swallows in my nest boxes and the song sparrows that nest beneath the tangle of dead maple branches that I never get around to removing. Each May I must carefully work around buried, fur-lined rabbit nests, and at midmonth the first young woodchucks will be poking their heads above ground to see what the world looks like.

There are never enough days in May, so the trick is to make the most of the 31 we get.

Songbird Migration

With May comes the great tide of north-bound songbirds, returning from their wintering grounds in the tropics. While many stay in my area to breed, still others—bay-breasted and blackpoll warblers, yellow-bellied flycatchers, and the like—will push on hundreds of miles into Canada. Their presence, however transitory, unites my home with the rain forests and the Far North.

Sky Watch

Eta Aquarid meteor shower: May 4
First quarter: May 7
Full moon: May 14
Last quarter: May 21
New moon: May 29

Most songbirds (robins and hummingbirds are two exceptions) migrate at night, taking advantage of the cooler, calmer air, and using the day to feed. The flocks are most active—and easiest to see—for an hour or two after dawn, foraging and singing as they continue to move north, one tree at a time.

Any wooded area is likely to be good for spring migrants, although forests along the shores of large lakes, rivers, and streams are often the best. City parks—oases amid the development—can be exceptional for bird watching, as are old urban cemeteries with their groves of stately trees.

Journal Notes

- **1** First Canada goose goslings and mallard chicks hatch; first tiger swallowtail butterflies emerge, having overwintered in chrysalids. New deer antlers begin showing as small knobs on bucks.
- **3** Ruby-throated hummingbirds arrive from tropics; clean and fill feeders by the time the lilacs bloom.
- **4** Robin eggs starting to hatch; pink lady's-slipper orchids in bloom.
- **6** Peak of spring songbird migration; best viewing shortly after dawn in wooded areas.
- **9** Wild dogwood blooming; killdeer chicks hatching.
- **12** Baby woodchucks first appear above ground; baby gray squirrels first seen outside dens.
- **15** Blue-eyed grass and fringed polygala blooming.
- **18** Orioles building nests. To help them, hang in trees mesh or wire baskets filled with 6-inch lengths of string or yarn. Pull some strands out so they dangle; this attracts the female oriole's attention.
- **20** Wild azalea reaches peak.
- **23** Black raspberries in full bloom; check back in early July for berries.
- **26** Mountain laurel begins flowering; first turkey and grouse chicks hatching.
- **31** Fireflies appear; first wild strawberries ripen.

JUNE

Ah, June. Hot enough to be summer when you're working in the garden at noon, but often chilly enough at night that the flannel sheets still feel good. It's a month that slows the headlong rush of May into something more stately and resonant, when the light lingers so long into evening that night seems like a memory.

June brings its share of muggy, hazy days, but there's usually a clarity to a June day that defies description—a deeper blue to the sky, a richer green on the hills. The roadsides are spangled with oxeye daisies and the orange of day lilies, but in the woods the carpets of wildflowers have faded beneath the deep shade of mature tree leaves. Wherever there's a gap in the canopy, though, the mountain laurel shimmers with pink and white, and by the end of the month the rhododendrons are blooming in the damp shade beneath the hemlocks. Meanwhile, the air in the valleys has the sharp, lovely smell of fresh-cut hay, and the clattering sound of balers echoes over the fields.

This is the month when the rewards for all your labors start coming to the table: strawberries and lettuce, peas and radishes, rhubarb and spinach, the vanguard of the garden's bounty.

Backyard Butterflies

Just as flowers and birds appear each year on my property, so do butterflies. I may see a dark mourning cloak on a mild winter day, but the first reliable sightings will be in April and May, when spring azures—tiny, sky-blue creatures—tiger swallowtails, and pearl crescents show up, having emerged from their chrysalids or other hiding spots where they spent the winter.

By June my backyard butterfly palette includes black and spicebush swallowtails, clouded sulfurs, red-spotted purples, and the very first monarchs, which have migrated north from the southern states. I've planted my garden with them in mind, including lots of good nectaring sources. Sprawling butterfly bushes are always the most popular stop, but many native plants provide abundant nectar, such as swamp (or red) milkweed and orange butterfly milkweed, several varieties of yellow coreopsis, and the lower-growing rose coreopsis. Later in the summer, my Joe-Pye weed, various asters and goldenrods, bee balm, and phlox are all popular with the butterflies.

I've also started gardening with an eye toward the caterpillars. I find the small, sluglike larvae of the spring azures on my viburnums, and the lush carpet of violets in the shady beds always means plenty of variegated fritillaries.

Sky Watch

First quarter: June 6
Full moon: June 13
Last quarter: June 19
Summer solstice: June 21
New moon: June 28

Journal Notes

1 Middle of fawning season for white-tailed deer.

3 Peak of the nesting season for songbirds.

9 Gray tree frogs calling from shrubs around woodland ponds, an explosive trill. Painted turtles laying eggs in sunny spots on pond banks.

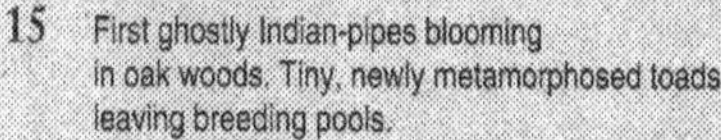

15 First ghostly Indian-pipes blooming in oak woods. Tiny, newly metamorphosed toads leaving breeding pools.

18 Day lilies begin blooming; unopened buds can be boiled lightly, then buttered and eaten.

22 Starlings form large flocks—earliest sign of autumn. Shadbush berries ripe and ready to eat.

24 Box turtles laying eggs. The female scoops out a deep hole with her hind legs, lays a half-dozen eggs, covers them, and leaves the warm earth to incubate them.

26 Red, furry seed heads of staghorn sumac ripening. Steep them in cold water for several hours, strain them through a clean cloth to remove hairs, and sweeten them to make pink "lemonade."

30 Orange butterfly milkweed opening, a favorite nectar plant of butterflies.

JULY

July is the month when thunderstorms roll across a landscape of solid green. It is a month of rocketing corn and stultifying heat, a time when the sparkle of fireflies at dusk echoes the flickering of distant lightning on the horizon.

Even here in the mountains, July can be a cauldron. A heat wave in June usually lacks the ferocity of one in July, when a big high pressure cell settles in over Bermuda and begins pumping up a merciless stream of haze and humidity. The hills disappear behind a cottony white murk, and the bluebirds sit, open-mouthed, in the tepid trickle of the waterfall, almost too tired to take a bath.

Sky Watch

First quarter: July 5
Full moon: July 12
Last quarter: July 19
New moon: July 27
Delta Aquarid meteor shower: July 30

Living as I do surrounded by open fields, July thunderstorms always test my nerves. But it is invariably moving to see the great towers of cloud, black-bottomed and white-topped, come roaring down upon me with their attendant winds and flashes, leaving a fresh-scrubbed world in their violent wake.

Journal Notes

3 Black raspberries ripe—if you can beat the birds to them.

6 Barn swallows starting to flock; immatures (told by paler undersides) sunbathe each morning on my porch roof just outside my office windows.

12 Second (or in some cases, third) clutches of bluebird eggs hatching.

15 First murmurings of summer insect choir: katydids, tree crickets, field crickets. Dewberries ripening.

17 Deer antlers, encased in velvety, blood-rich skin, growing rapidly all month. By late July the rack's basic size and form are determined.

23 Blackberries ripening in fencerows, highbush blueberries in mountain bogs. First southbound shorebirds migrating from Arctic.

27 Wet-meadow wildflowers like blue vervain, ironweed, and boneset opening.

Eating Out

Everyone agrees there's a growing rift between people and the land, but one of the most enjoyable ways to bridge that gap is by eating wild foods—and summer is a berry-picker's delight.

In June the wild strawberries ripen, followed by the shadbush berries. But the pace quickens in July, when a succession of delicious edibles come into season. First are the black raspberries, whose globular fruits start red and ripen to a lustrous indigo-black in early July. In the next weeks come the smaller dewberries, the Asian wineberries (which grow wild in many areas), the large, heavily seeded blackberries, and the red raspberries.

And that's only what you can find along roadsides and old fencerows. In July the various species of wild blueberries are ripe, and picking them is a country tradition in many regions. Drier woods—especially areas that have been burned or logged in decades past—are the places to look for black huckleberries, which grow on low shrubs, while cool, boggy patches host the big highbush blueberry bushes, often 10 or 15 feet tall and loaded with berries.

AUGUST

August is a ripe month, a settled, steady, somnolent month. The landscape begins to change hue in August, from the deep green of July to a golden, burnished color that comes from the corn tassels and drying grass heads.

We consider this a summer month, but wildlife knows otherwise. The signs of autumn are there if you know where to look: The first black gum leaves are turning red, and the first hawks and eagles are drifting south whenever a cold front sends north winds whistling through the haze. The songbirds no longer contest territorial boundaries with each other, but gather in congenial flocks, the friction of the breeding season forgotten.

The land is never so full of life as it is in August. After months of relentless (almost reckless) procreation, the world is spilling over with birds and mammals and insects and flowers and everything else, an absolute extravagance of living. In the months ahead nature will pare that excess down to the bone, but for now I revel in a sense of a land bursting at the seams.

The Noisy Nights of August

Friends came to visit from the city a few years ago, and dinner stretched into evening as we sat on the patio. As full dark came, one of them asked how I could sleep with all the racket. I had to think, just for a moment, before I realized she meant the insects.

Late summer days are quiet, the birds having ceased their breeding songs, but the August nights erupt with sound. I love the surge and ebb of the layered noise—the racheting creak of the katydids asking their endless question, and answering it themselves, *Katydid? Katydidn't. Katydid? Katydidn't.* The big field crickets, shining black when I roust them from the flower beds in daylight, whittle away through their chirps, while from the trees and grass the snowy tree crickets keep up their metronomic pulse of notes, so precise you can use them as a thermometer.

Like most animals, insects sing for sex. Some hear those songs with membranes stretched across holes in their body wall, others with "ears" in their legs. Their voices are not artifacts of breath and throat, but the result of scraping and sawing or rubbing wing against wing, or wing against leg. It may seem strange to us, but they were doing it long before we arrived—and anyone listening on a warm August night knows it works.

Sky Watch

First quarter: August 4
Full moon: August 10
Perseid meteor shower: August 11
Last quarter: August 18
New moon: August 26

Journal Notes

6 Goldenrod opening (blame the ragweed for your hay fever, not the innocent goldenrod).

15 Autumn hawk migration begins midmonth with first bald eagles heading south. Box turtle eggs hatching.

17 Watch courtship displays of short-horned grasshoppers—brief flights with snapping, crackling wingbeats—along country roads.

21 Month when most snake eggs hatch. Some species, like female garter snakes, give birth to live young late this month. Elderberries ripening.

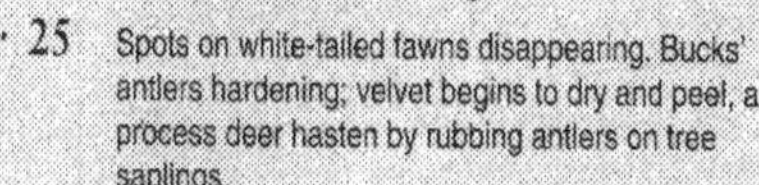

25 Spots on white-tailed fawns disappearing. Bucks' antlers hardening; velvet begins to dry and peel, a process deer hasten by rubbing antlers on tree saplings.

30 Peak of monarch butterfly migration; most will travel to highlands of central Mexico for the winter. Migration starts in early August and continues through late September.

SEPTEMBER

The world shakes itself awake in September, as though it suddenly realizes how much it has to accomplish before winter sets in. There is a frenzy to autumn that begins in earnest now, as cold fronts start their march from the Arctic, blowing away the muggy August air like a slap across the face.

The fall migration of birds actually begins in late July with the first southbound shorebirds, but this month the migration becomes evident to even the most unobservant person. At dusk the trees in back yards, parks, and woodlots flicker with the movement of small birds—warblers, vireos, tanagers, orioles, and others, all preparing for a night of travel. They gorge on insects and berries; each September the robins move, en masse, into my crab apples and clean them out in a day, fueling up for their long flight south.

Nor are birds the only migrants. Monarch butterflies headed for Mexico pause to sip from the goldenrod in my meadow, and red bats—some traveling as far south as Central America—pass through here this month and next, tying the hemispheres together with their wanderings.

Getting Ready for Winter

Nature weaves a tapestry of movement and preparation each autumn. Some of the scenes are grand, like that of birds and butterflies traveling thousands of miles. Others are so subtle that you can miss them in your own back yard.

Each September I find female mantises creating their bizarre egg masses wherever vegetation is thick. Some are the elongated cases of the small, native Carolina mantis, but most are the big flattened globes of the praying mantis, a European import. Last year I watched a female praying mantis laying her eggs; she extruded what looked just like insulation foam, a frothy, yellow-brown substance that quickly dried to a hard, impervious case. Deep inside, protected from wind and cold, were the eggs.

Journal Notes

1 Painted turtle eggs hatching; young may stay in nest over winter and not emerge until spring.

3 Female timber rattlesnakes giving birth, often in the company of other pregnant females at traditional birthing sites.

5 Watch for clouds of migrating green darner dragonflies; millions were spotted in the autumn of 1993 across the Northeast and Midwest.

10 Yellows and purples dominate the meadow as New England asters and ironweed bloom amid a sea of goldenrod.

15 Sweet birches turning yellow on the drier hillsides, black gum leaves turning red.

17 Peak of broad-winged hawk migration in Northeast. Some hawkwatch locations have recorded more than 20,000 in a single day; bald eagles, ospreys, and kestrels also migrating.

25 Woolly bear caterpillars crawling everywhere this month and in early October, looking for sheltered spots to pass the winter.

30 First frost; best time to pick wild fox grapes.

Sky Watch

First quarter: September 2
Full moon: September 9
Last quarter: September 16
Autumnal equinox: September 23
New moon: September 24

The chokecherries and sassafras trees along the road west of the house are full of frantic caterpillars this month—the big, green larvae of promethea moths, one of the most common of the huge silkmoths. Fully grown the caterpillars are 2 to 3 inches long, with red and blue tubercles down their backs like clown paint. Fat and ready for winter, they wrap themselves in a rolled leaf, cocoon that within a shell of silk, and sleep through the winter. Come spring, those that the chickadees miss will emerge as moths as big as a child's hand.

OCTOBER

Everyone has their favorite month. Beachgoers revel in July's sun, gardeners love June's blossoms, and skiers crave the snows of January. For me, though, October is the best of the year—I love the scratch of a wool sweater, the taste of tart apples, the sight of ragged clouds in a chilly sky, and the annual spectacle of changing leaves that never fails to render me speechless.

October's intensity is also breathtaking—the feeling of a season running at full throttle. This is not a peaceful, serene month, but one that for all its pageantry and beauty is unsettling. We may live lives that are sadly divorced from the natural world, but in October our subconscious senses the same thing the migrating geese and the denning woodchucks know: Winter is approaching.

It may be this disquieting edge that gives October its special shine. A primitive part of us shivers with that knowledge, even as we admire the flaming hillsides and orange pumpkins.

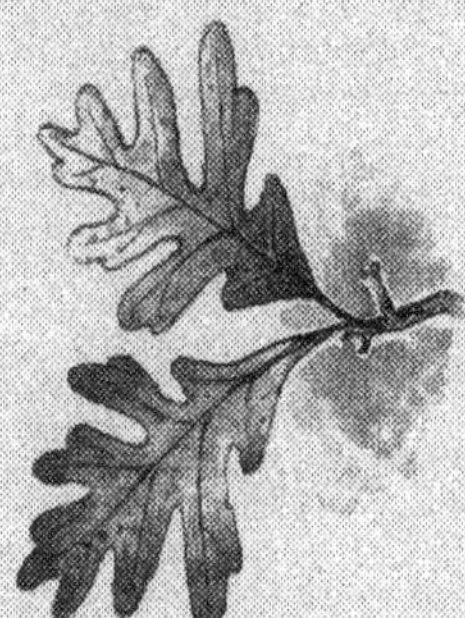

October Colors

Science has learned a good deal about *how* leaves turn color in the fall, but we still know relatively little about *why*. For most trees, it seems to be almost accidental—a result of the chemical changes necessary for winter.

Some of a leaf's colors, especially the yellows and browns, were there all summer, masked by the green of chlorophyll, which is withdrawn from the leaf as fall approaches. Others, like the intense reds and oranges, are produced as sugars trapped within the dying leaves are chemically broken down. That's why weather is so important to a good foliage display; warm days and cool (but not freezing) nights stimulate sugar production.

There may be no benefit to the trees in all turning brilliant colors at once, but biologists now realize that some of the earliest species to turn, like black gum, spicebush, and dogwood, may be advertising. These trees change a week or two before the rest of the forest, just when their abundant, fat-rich fruits are ripening. The red or yellow leaves may serve as a signal for birds loading up on food before migrating—and in return, the birds will scatter the trees' seeds far and wide in their droppings.

Sky Watch

First quarter: October 1
Full moon: October 8
Draconid meteor shower: October 9
Last quarter: October 16
Orionid meteor shower: October 20
Taurid meteor shower: October 21
New moon: October 24
First quarter: October 30

Journal Notes

1 "Crazy flight" time for ruffed grouse and bobwhite, when young birds looking for new territories end up in unlikely places, like suburbs and cities.

5 Peak migration of sharp-shinned hawks and falcons. Maples at their richest color.

8 American painted lady and buckeye butterflies are moving south—not true migrants, since they will not return in spring.

12 First juncos and white-throated sparrows appear at feeder.

14 Oaks at peak color, turning ridges orange and bronze.

20 Leaves starting to fall, creating cascades of color.

22 Green frogs disappearing from sight, entering hibernation on bottoms of ponds, lakes, and marshes.

28 Mountains bare of leaves; only color is yellow of tulip-trees along streams and springs, making gold threads up the ridges.

NOVEMBER

November has a forgotten, neglected look to it. The naked trees, the browning grass, the purple bramble canes, and old, weathered weed stalks along the roads all give this month a forlorn air.

Oddly, I think November is at its best on a drizzly day. Rain darkens the tree trunks, lending them the look of ancient columns, and gives the fallen leaves a shimmer. The flat light from the overcast sky gentles the landscape, and the damp air heightens aromas that you'd miss on a dry, breezy day. There is the tang of the oak leaves, a scent that takes most of us back to childhood games in leaf piles; there's the smell of earth, a touch of woodsmoke, and just a hint of the cold to come.

Disappearing Act

A few years ago, on a sunny day in late November, a weasel bounded across the back yard while I was planting bulbs—a snowy white animal with a black tail tip.

The weasel's white coat was stunning, but as camouflage it was a spectacular failure, since we'd had no snow yet. Our Pennsylvania winters are fickle that way, which might explain why only a small percentage of weasels around here turn white in winter, while most of those farther north do. For some reason, in areas where only part of the population changes, more often it is the males that turn white.

Researchers have shown that the length of day, not temperature or snowfall, triggers the change. The hairs themselves do not turn colors, however; instead, the shorter days cause the pigment-producing cells to shut down, so that newly grown hairs come in white, replacing old, brown hairs that have molted. Starting around mid-March the process reverses, with new brown hairs growing in.

Sky Watch

Full moon: November 7
Andromedid meteor shower: November 14
Last quarter: November 15
Leonid meteor shower: November 16
New moon: November 22
First quarter: November 29

Journal Notes

1 Chipmunks and woodchucks usually disappear into winter dens about now. Woodchucks enter profound sleep, but chipmunks wake often to feed from food caches, and may even come above ground.

6 Little brown bats gathering at traditional hibernation sites, usually caves or old mine shafts. May hunt for bugs on warm evenings near cave mouth.

9 Pregnant female black bears denning up early this month; males and barren females wait until beginning of December.

12 Most white-tailed bucks now entering rut, or breeding season, which lasts about two weeks. Worst time of year for deer-car collisions as bucks throw caution to the wind.

17 Look in old meadows for goldenrod galls—thumb-sized swellings on stems that hide tiny fly larvae through the winter.

20 Witch hazel in bloom, bearing small, scraggly yellow flowers with the faint scent of flowing stream water.

25 Deer mice and white-footed mice busy roofing over old bird's nests with grass and plant fluff to make weatherproof food caches for seeds and berries, or even for use as cozy dens.

30 Ruffed grouse growing comblike scales on toes, which will act as snowshoes through the winter.

DECEMBER

Through November the days grow shorter so quickly you can almost feel it, but by December the erosion of daylight slows, bottoming out. The world itself eases to a crawl, and we try to hide this fact with our holiday bustle. No wonder we feel hassled and tired, as our bodies—and the natural world—try to tell us to take it easy while we push even harder.

There is an elegance to December that transcends holidays. This is the month when this area's first snows arrive, burying the flaws of tattered autumn.

With the passing of the holidays, when we finally take a moment to think about it, comes the realization that the solstice has come and gone, too. Earth has passed one of its four great milestones of the year, and for the next six months each day will be just a little bit brighter than the one before. December's message, buried deep within its snows, is always one of renewal.

Sky Watch

Full moon: December 7
Geminid meteor shower: December 13
Last quarter: December 15
Winter solstice: December 22
New moon: December 22
First quarter: December 28

In the Deep Freeze

When the temperature plummets, birds can migrate and mammals can grow an extra-thick layer of fur and fat. But how do such seemingly fragile animals as frogs and insects make it through winter?

Many reptiles and amphibians dig below the frost line—in the mud bottoms of ponds, in jumbled rock slides on mountains, or in old mammal burrows. But some frogs, like spring peppers and gray tree frogs, crawl only a few inches below the soil line, where temperatures drop well below zero.

They protect themselves by filling their cells with a syrupy chemical called glycerol, which keeps ice crystals from forming inside the cells themselves. Some insects also use glycerol in their tissues, while others rely on special proteins that encourage ice to form in the minute spaces between cells, rather than inside them.

Journal Notes

3 Rutting season ending for deer; most doe have mated and will have twins next spring.

7 Flying squirrels setting up housekeeping in bird boxes; several may jam into one box, sharing their warmth.

13 Life continues beneath the snow—mice and shrews share their tunnels with wolf spiders, mites, beetles, even hunting weasels.

18 Some painted turtles still active (although at a reduced level) beneath pond ice. Others hibernating in muddy bottoms.

21 White-tailed bucks begin losing their antlers.

23 In fields where farmers are spreading manure, look for snow buntings and horned larks searching for seeds.

26 On sunny days watch for snow fleas—minute insects called springtails that pepper the snow.

SPIRITUAL APPLICATION

Each changing season of my life reveals His presence.

In Charles Swindoll's book, *Growing Strong in the Seasons of Life*, Multnomah Press, he states:

> "I am glad God changes the times and the seasons, aren't you? Just think how dull things would become if He didn't paint nature's scenes in different colors several times a year. With infinite creativity and remarkable regularity, He splashes white over brown and orange over green, giving such attention to detail that we are often stunned with amazement.
>
> "Each of the four seasons offers fresh and vital insights for those who take the time to look and to think. Hidden beneath the surface are colorful yet silent truths that touch almost every area across the landscape of our lives. As each three-month segment of every year holds its own mysteries and plays its own melodies, offering sights and smells, feelings and fantasies, altogether distinct, so it is in the seasons of life. The Master is neither mute nor careless as He alters our times and changes our seasons. How wrong to trudge blindly and routinely through a lifetime of changing seasons without discovering answers to the new mysteries and learning to sing the new melodies! Seasons are designed to deepen us, to instruct us in the

wisdom and ways of our God. To help us grow strong...like a tree planted by the rivers of water.

"Our journey begins in the winter, a season of quiet *reverence.* This is followed by spring, a season of refreshing and encouraging *renewal.* Then comes summer, a season of enjoyable and much-needed *rest.* Finally, we'll stroll through autumn, a season of nostalgic *reflection.* Our hope is to grow stronger and taller as our roots dig deeper in the soft soil along the banks of the river of life. And let's not fear the winds of adversity! The gnarled old twisted trees, beaten and buffeted by wind and weather along the ocean shores, tell their own stories of consistent courage. May God make us strong as the winds whip against us, my friend. Roots grow deep when the winds are strong. Let's commit ourselves to growing strong in the seasons of life."

Oswald Chambers muses, "We may ask, 'Why does God bring thunderclouds and disasters when we want green pastures and still waters?' Bit by bit, we find behind the clouds the Father's feet; behind the lightning an abiding day that has no night, behind the thunder, a still, small voice that comforts with a comfort that is unspeakable." (Adapted from *The Place of Help.*)

Isaiah 43:2-3 reads, "When you pass through the waters, I will be with you, and when you pass through the rivers, they will not sweep over you. When you walk through the fire you will not be burned; the flames will not set you ablaze. For I am the Lord, your God, the Holy One of Israel, your Savior."

Gigi Graham Tchividjian, in *Weather of the Heart* states, "Make the least of all that goes and the most of all that comes. Don't regret what is past. Cherish what you have. Look forward to all that is to come and most important of all, rely moment by moment on Jesus Christ."

Taking from Swindoll's *Growing Strong in the Seasons of Life* again, one chapter is entitled "A Way in the Storm."

> "Blow that layer of dust off the book of Nahum in your Bible and catch a glimpse of the last part of verse 3, chapter 1: 'The way of the Lord is in the whirlwind and in the storm...'
>
> "That's good to remember when you're in a rip-snortin', Texas frog-strangler as I was a few weeks back. I nudged myself to remember God's presence as the rain-heavy, charcoal clouds hemorrhaged in eerie, aerial explosions of saw-toothed lightning and reverberating thunder. Witnessing that atmospheric drama, I reminded myself of its Director who was once again, having His way in the whirlwind and the storm. Nahum and I took the Texas highway through Weatherford, Cisco, Abilene, and Sweetwater. There was no doubt but that the Lord, the God of the heavens, was in the storm. Nature refuses to let you forget her Artist.
>
> "But life too has its storms. Hurricanes that descend from blue, sun-drenched skies, or clear, starry nights. What about the whirlwinds of disease, disaster, and death?

What about the storms of interruptions, irritations, and ill treatment? If Nahum's words apply to the heavenly sphere, do they also apply to the earthly? Surely, if God's way is in the murky, threatening sky, it is also in the difficult, heart-straining contingencies of daily living. The Director of the heavenly and earthly theaters is One..and the same. The cast may be different, the plot may be altered, the props may be rearranged, but just offstage stands the Head, the Chief...overseeing every act, every scene, every line.

"Ask Nebuchadnezzar. He would reply: 'And all the inhabitants of the earth are accounted as nothing, but He does according to His will in the host of heaven and among the inhabitants of earth; and no one can ward off His hand or say to Him, "What has Thou done?' (Daniel 4:35)

"David, if asked, would answer: 'But our God is in the heavens; He does whatever He pleases.' (Psalm 115:3).

"Paul would add: 'For it is God who is at work in you, both to will and to work for His good pleasure.' (Philippians 2:13)

"Moses nailed it down with his comment: 'When you are in distress and all these things have come upon you...you will return to the Lord your God and listen to His voice.' (Deuteronomy 4:30)

> "Life is literally filled with God-appointed storms. It would take several volumes much bulkier than this one to list the whirlwinds in the walk of a Christian. But two things should comfort us in the midst of daily lightning and thunder, and rain, and wind. First, these squalls surge across *everyone's* horizon. God has no favorite actors who always get the leading role. Second, we all *need* them. God has no other method more effective. The massive blows and shattering blasts (not to mention the little, constant irritations) smooth us, humble us, and compel us to submit to *His* script and *His* chosen role for our lives.
>
> "Before the dust settles, why not ask God to have His way in today's whirlwind. The play is so much more enjoyable when the cast cooperates with the Director."

Day 18 of *Quiet Times for Mothers*, by Julia Graham, is titled "Walk Cheerfully," and contains many quotes which address "weather" in our lives. It starts with Proverbs 23:7, "For as he thinketh within himself, so is he..."

"A vexation arises, and our expressions of impatience hinder others from taking it patiently. Disappointment, ailment, or even weather depresses us–and our look or tone of depression hinders others from maintaining a cheerful and thankful spirit. Wrong feeling is even more infectious than wrongdoing, especially the various phases of ill temper–gloominess, touchiness, discontentedness, irritability. Do we not know how *catching* these are." Frances Ridley Havergal

"All encounters in life, every personality, every institution, every relationship, is a mixture of the good and the bad. When we habitually focus on the bad, we are training ourselves in negativism. There is a secret cost in such an outlook to one's spiritual and mental health. In my case I woke up twenty years into adulthood to find myself deeply schooled in serious negativism. That, in turn, can bathe all of life in emotional gloom. When the habit continues...the dark glasses of criticalness can lead to long periods of melancholy and even to serious depression." - Catherine Marshall

"I find that it is not the circumstances in which we are placed, but the spirit in which we meet them, that constitutes our comfort–and this comfort may be undisturbed, if we seek for and cherish a feeling of quiet submission, whatever may come to us." - Elizabeth T. King (adapted)

"We are in danger of forgetting that God is not only a comfort but a joy. He is the source of all pleasures; He is fun and light and laughter, and we are meant to enjoy Him... *'Thou shall not enjoy life'* was never Christ's teaching... To be Christian is to be reborn, and free, and unafraid, and immortally young." - Joy Davidman

In regard to light, Ephesians 5:8-14 states "You were once darkness but now you are light in the Lord. Live as children of light." Light is a creation of God (Genesis 1:8-19), and He said it would serve as signs to mark seasons and days and years (NIV). He also said (Matthew 5:14) that we are the light of the world. And in verse 16 to let that light shine before men. And (Matthew 6:22) that if the light in us is darkness then that darkness is great (darkness is the absence of truth).

Why don't we shine? We eclipse. What is an eclipse? It's when there is an interference between the natural way the moon and the sun relate to each other. The deceptions of Satan (his #1 tactic) get in the way of the relationship we have with the Son. We don't want people to really know how we're doing, and the defects in our character. We make excuses. We have a lack of integrity. We justify our opinions so we can't receive truth.

How can I walk in light? Recognize there's a deceiver. Combat deception. Get in the Word. Get wise and spiritual counsel, (counsel means being steered or guided by a rope: submissiveness). Be accountable. Listen to God's voice. He speaks truth. Know the difference. His spirit lives in us. God intends for us to walk in light, not darkness.

Notes

CHAPTER THIRTEEN

DISEASES

Source: University of Tennessee Agricultural Extension Service, *2002 Insect and Plant Disease Control Manual,* PB 1690 (Paraphrased)

Fungi, bacteria and nematodes found in soil are an indication of disease which can damage your plants and trees. Leaf spots and blights are caused by fungi and/or bacteria.

Diseases occur only when a susceptible host plant comes in contact with a pathogen (disease producing bacterium or microorganism) under favorable weather conditions. Diseases may not kill an entire plant, but may stunt its growth, reduce uniformity and plant quality. Diseases often result in increased expenses due to the cost of pesticides, labor, and dead plants. Diseased plants may introduce new pathogens to your landscape.

A symptom is the physical expression of disease by a plant. Disease symptoms include cankers, galls, leaf spots, rotted roots, wilting, etc. Signs are the actual part of the pathogen that are visible to the naked eye such as mushrooms, masses of fungal or bacterial spores, fruiting bodies of the fungi, etc.

Bacterial diseases may be spread by rain, insects, animals, or people. Examples include crown gall of euonymus, fire blight of crabapple and pear, shot hole of almond and peach, leaf spot of English ivy and cherry laurel, and soft roots and leaf scorch of shade trees.

Fungi are plants that lack chlorophyll and are not capable of manufacturing their own food as green plants do. Most are microscopic and multicellular plants with no roots, stem, or leaves. Some live on rotting plant debris or other dead food substances. These fungi are parasites. Examples are root rot of rhododendron; web blight; black root rot of Japanese holly; black spot of roses; spot anthracnose of dogwood; cedar apple rust and powdery mildew.

A root knot nematode is a microscopic round worm that usually feeds on plant roots and occasionally on foliage. The injury it causes interferes with the movement of minerals, nutrients and water into plant tissue. Roots damaged by nematodes may be more susceptible to fungal and bacterial diseases. These nematodes insert a spear-like mouthpiece into the plant to feed, some from outside the root, going into plant tissue.

Plant viruses are very tiny particles which can multiply only inside living cells. They are so small that they cannot be seen with ordinary light microscopes. Infected plants may become yellow and stunted or display twisted growth. Some viruses are spread by propagating diseased stock plants. Rose mosaic on hybrid tea roses is an example.

Disease management is based on knowledge of biological, environmental, cultural, genetic, and economic factors. Pesticides should only be used to complement other management practices such as avoidance, exclusion, eradication, and biological control.

Avoidance in choosing planting sites known to be free of certain pests or conditions that favor diseases, like using sterilized or soil-less or composted bark growing mixes free of, or with low levels of, soil-borne pathogens; not planting azalea, hybrid rhododendron, juniper, or yew in poorly drained clay soils that favor development of root rot; locating plum or cherry field blocks in areas of black cherry that are infected with black know; spacing plants to encourage good air movement to dry foliage and discourage foliar diseases; controlling irrigation frequency and quantity which can influence diseases such as root rots favored by excess water and fungal cankers; the use of sterilized pots, flats and propagating mix; managing insects which may spread disease; pull weeds which decrease air movement and compete for water and nutrients.

Exclusion is the inspecting of plant material and rejecting that which is infected before it enters the garden.

Eradication is eliminating disease after it is established by the use of crop rotation, letting the soil stay fallow to allow greater heating and drying, using clear plastic to solarize and raise the soil temperatures, and the use of fumigation.

Biological control can involve the use of disease-resistant cultivars.

Chemical control should be used as a last resort, because it can destroy helpful insects and, actually, most chemicals have not been proven to always eliminate disease inside a plant.

Fungicides used as foliar sprays can control diseases such as powdery mildew, rusts, or leaf spots, and to control stem and root rots. Prolonged use may not be effective as the fungi may become tolerant of the fungicide.

Identification of a plant's disease or disorder is important prior to treatment so the correct management strategies can be employed. Samples of diseased specimens should be taken to your local Extension office for the agent to identify, or if they are unable to do so they can send the specimen to their local Plant and Pest Diagnostic Center for identification.

SPIRITUAL APPLICATION

I can do all things through Him who strengthens me.

In *A Life Worth Living,* Nick Gumbel has written, "No sin can be conquered, or anything with lasting worth accomplished without His help; we have to cooperate with the spirit of God in all that we do. In gardening, the growth comes from the plant itself, but the gardener has a vital role to play. So it is with our spiritual lives: God gives the growth, we tend the plant. God's work in us includes our wills. He works in us to will and act according to His good purpose (Philippians 4:13). Many fear to trust God with their future because they fear that God will make them do something they have no desire to do, or that He will make a mess of their lives. Both of these fears are without foundation. If our wills are surrendered to His will God will give us the desire to do whatever He is calling us to do. If He calls us to a ministry to the poor, that is where the person's heart will be. If He calls us to a teaching work, He will give us the desire to teach. If we surrender to His will, He will work out His good purpose. What He wants for our lives is good. It will not necessarily be easy. But we will not be able to improve on His plan; in fact, working out our salvation means fulfilling our potential as the whole person we were created to be."

Patsy Clairmont has said, "Something liberating and healing happens when we relinquish our right to understand God's requests. Such joy can come over us that it's all we can do not to shout."

In reading the University of Tennessee text about plant diseases, I see parallels relating to spiritual diseases. Taking the paragraphs in order, here's what I see, noting that sin can be a disease, but not all disease is sin.

Diseases have symptoms; visible signs. The book of Proverbs is a wonderful guide to define sin, which, in some cases, as stated above, can be a disease, i.e., sexual addiction, or pathological lying.

When spiritual disease is present in a person, certain incidents or contacts may trigger its activity. A person may be physically, emotionally and spiritually limited because of these actions. Re-reading the practical text with this in mind can give insight into how these diseases continue and breed. Psalm 119, verses 105, 130 and 133, instruct how the Word of God brings understanding. Awareness of our frailties and weaknesses can go a long way toward overcoming and eradicating conditions which limit us as Christians. Read Proverbs 1:7, Hosea 4:6, Proverbs 24:4, Proverbs 2:10, and Proverbs 7:12 for additional understanding.

Avoid people, places, and things which bring out weaknesses (exercising discipline). Exclude them from your life. Clean your home, place of work, and any surroundings under your control, of materials which can weaken your discipline.

Examples of healings done by Jesus may be found by reading Mark 1:21-28, Luke 4:38-41, Luke 5:12-13, Mark 1:40-45, Luke 5:18-26, Matthew 9:1-9, Mark 2:3, Matthew 9:27-31, Matthew 9:22-24, Mark 7:31-36, Matthew 20:29-34, Luke 18:35-43, and Matthew 9:17-23.

Our pastor, Steve Streeter, shared that "the image of who you are in Christ will determine what you do in the Kingdom."

Pete Rose, former baseball player for the Cincinnati Reds, ruined his good fame by gambling. He wrote a book about his failure. Mike Lopresti, a sportswriter for Gannett News Service wrote about Rose, "If there is still pride within him, no amount of book royalties will ever make the pain go away, knowing he will always be remembered for what he became as much as what he was."

Leviticus 26:44 states, "No matter what you have done I am still the Lord your God, and I will never completely reject you or become absolutely disgusted with you there in the land of your enemies."

In our local newspaper, *The Daily Times*, Pastor Dave Anderson reflects on man being created in the image of God, stating that the Lord has placed certain things within mankind that mirror some of His attributes and which must be construed as an expression of the image of God. He states that our minds are sensitive to truth and untruth, attracted to beauty, our curiosity is endless. Ecclesiastes 3:22, states that 'He has put eternity into man's heart, yet so that he cannot find out what God has done from the beginning to the end." Pastor Anderson thinks the writer of Ecclesiastes suggests very strongly that the unexplained hunger for the divine is both very legitimate and profoundly important, and that there is a reason for our fascination with life beyond the grave, time beyond our times, matters which are beyond our grasp, yet planted deeply within our consciousness. He states, "They are engraved upon our very soul as a designed way of thinking," and goes on to write, "The Bible explains that for us, and offers a remedy for the hunger of man's soul. That remedy is Jesus, the Son of God, who came to live among us, and spilled His blood to redeem His people. He promised us that He would come again for us, and take us to be with Him forever. Eternity then, is a very serious question for all of us, and a most precious one of those who belong to Christ."

He continues, "The Bible tells us certain things we should believe about God, and certain duties which God requires of man. It teaches us to trust Jesus. It tells us that He promised to come again, to take us to be with Him. Jesus assures those who love Him that He will not leave them as orphans, that He will come to them, that He is the resurrection and the life, and that whoever believes in Him will never die."

Pastor Anderson concludes, "We are not given the option of not choosing. Either we entrust our soul to the 'nothing,' or we entrust our soul to the salvation which our creator God has provided for us, by faith in his Son, Jesus Christ. There is an element of the image of God in you, designed into the deepest codes of your being. The 'Unknown' is not just the nothing. It is really a very important Something."

Exodus 15:26 states, "If you listen carefully to the voice of the Lord your God and do what is right in His eyes, if you pay attention to His commands and keep all His decrees, I will not bring on you any of the diseases I brought on the Egyptians, for I am the Lord who heals you."

Notes

CHAPTER FOURTEEN

WHAT CAN THE LORD DO WITH MY WILDERNESS?

In 1993, when Ted and I were looking for property where we could live and take care of my mother when she needed us, we walked over 11.3 acres outside of Maryville, Tennessee, near the little Tennessee River. The property was so overgrown with weeds, brambles, blackberries, and scrub pines we had a hard time defining the topography of the front five acres. And back in the six acres of woods, honeysuckle vines and poison ivy were strangling some of the trees so much they looked like they would die. Fallen trees from storms had knocked over other trees like dominos, and walking through the area was difficult.

We carried Mother's hoe and a big stick to hit the ground to scare away any snakes which we obviously could not see at our feet. We'd walk a little way and hit a bramble patch and have to go in another direction. And yet, we could see that the property really had potential.We bought it and dedicated it to the Lord for His use. Then I started dreaming about what to do with it.

Each time we vacationed in Tennessee, until May of 1999 when we moved here, I prayed, planned, and designed.

We got acquainted with some of the neighbors, and one summer, when we came to Tennessee for a vacation, the neighbor on the north mowed it all, to surprise us, and then we saw what the Lord had blessed us with. It was beautiful!

About a third of the trees in the woods were scrub

pines, some of them so small around, yet about 50 feet tall. But they were dead because they could not get light, and their roots could not get nourishment because of the crowding. Even though they were dead they could not fall over because they were so close together.

In November of 1999, we found loggers who removed all the "bad" pines, but they left quite a mess in the process. It took us four years to clean up all the branches and the small trees which they could not sell for pulp wood. We made arbors and fences from some of the salvage.

Today, it's a far cry from that first glimpse. It's cleaned, mowed, planted, and we live there in a beautiful home.

That's what happens to us when we allow the Lord to take our wildernesses and prepare us for His use.

Have you ever known someone whose life was a wilderness? Has yours ever been like that? Mine has, and I'm still in the process, with my Master Gardener cutting and pruning, mowing and weeding, digging out, planting and transplanting in my spiritual garden.

What causes wildernesses? Disobedience, ignorance, wrong teaching, being out from under God's protection because of willful sin, generational sin passed on from the life of our parents (Exodus 20:5, 34:7, Numbers 14:18, Deuteronomy 5:9), lack of prayer and fellowship with the Lord, to name a few.

Sometimes we get involved in activities which seem harmless at the time, but can begin to stifle us and take us away from the Lord. We begin to die. An example of vines which can kill plants and trees:

<u>Wisteria</u>. Beautiful, fragrant, covers over. Heavy vines which need lots of support. Roots reach out and sprout up in areas where you don't want them to grow. A part of the past, not submitted to the Lord since receiving salvation?

<u>Morning glory vine</u>. Beautiful, vivid colored flowers.

This vine is destructive. It saps life from the host plant. My life? What kind of "beauty" is sapping me? My companions who do not follow the Lord and therefore are a bad influence?

Kudzu. The fast-growing Kudzu was imported from Japan in 1911 to control erosion and restore nitrogen-depleted soil. The edible rootstocks and tough bark fibers were added benefits, and the leaves supplied fodder and chicken feed. But in the warm, wet climate of the Southeast, the Kudzu ran rampant, overgrowing forests, fields, and buildings at the rate of 100 feet a year and more. Today, the kudzu invasion is a serious problem throughout the region. In the south, you can see trees alongside the road which are dead with the vine all over them, as well as abandoned houses and vehicles. It can cover anything in a matter of days. No wonder it's called, "The vine that ate the South." Could this be an organization I joined thinking it would "enhance" me, but it is teaching me to compromise what the Word teaches me? (Freemasonry is a good example of this kind of group.)

Japanese honeysuckle. Climbing or trailing. Has flowers which turn yellow and are very fragrant, with tubular, backswept petals and showy stamens. Leaves are in pairs. Any child who has picked a honeysuckle blossom to taste the sweet nectar from its nipple-like base can appreciate the group's evocative name. There are many native North American species, but none is so widespread or pervasive as the imported Japanese honeysuckle. Introduced as a fragrant ornamental for screenings and trellises and used as a ground cover for road banks and other easily eroded sites, it soon outgrew its assigned role. With the help of birds that relish the small black fruits, the seeds have spread far and wide, producing tangled vines that have overgrown, and now threaten to strangle, whole forests in the East. This might be a church you have joined where the teachings are man's way of putting people in bondage to a pastor or organization. It seemed "sweet" at the outset but has really gotten off track from God's Word. (Remember Jim Jones and the people who were brainwashed to drink deadly poison?)

What can I do when I become aware of what a mess my life is?

Joshua 14:6.

1. Know what God has promised. (:6)
2. Be honest and faithful. (:7)
3. Be strong for whatever God calls you to do. (:11)
4. Take what is rightfully yours. (:12)
5. Reap the reward. (:13).

June Hunt, *Devotions From Godly Women*, Zondervan. 1 Corinthians 10:13. "When God fills your spirit with His spirit and infuses you with His strength, you are no longer captive to any temptation. Every can't becomes a can.

Deuteronomy 33:27 (GNB) "God has always been your defense. His eternal arms are your support. He drove out your enemies as you advanced and told you to destroy them all."

How do we destroy our enemies? The Holy Spirit can show us what (who) they are and expose them. It is then up to us to take authority over them through spiritual warfare, in the name of Jesus. We no longer allow them to have dominion and control in our lives. Greater is He who is in me that he who is in the world. (1John 4:4) Satan and his demons (my enemies) are under my feet. I have authority over them. I have no need to cower or be afraid; the Lord has given me the victory. He is my defense! Satan only has whatever power I allow him to have through fear and ignorance.

From a devotional by, Phyllis Vierheller, *Virtue* Magazine, July/August, 1988. "Old patterns are pinned to the fabric edges of my mind, Lord. Release the pins with your gentle fingers that my thoughts might flow freely in new designs of Your shaping."

Beverly La Haye, referring to 2 Timothy 1:7, "I began to realize that my fears and anxieties were self-imposed. God's choice for me was to have power, love and self-discipline. God did not give me a spirit of fear. My poor self image, my anxieties, my fears, were all my own doing and my sin, because I lacked faith to receive the power, love and self-discipline that God really wanted me to have."

Will our distresses drive us to despair and discouragement or to God? David encouraged himself in the Lord (1 Samuel 30:6).

I was recently reading my Bible's introduction to 1 Chronicles which states that one thing the book shows is that in spite of the disasters that had fallen on Israel and Judah, God was still keeping His promises and working out His plan for His people through those who were living in Judah. God shows His faithfulness regardless of our wilderness, if we're obedient to Him.

Women's Devotional New Testament, NIV, Zondervan. "**The Lord Hears."** Psalm 34 has been a source of strength and encouragement ever since I drank from the "living waters" of eternal salvation in Jesus Christ. Praising, glorifying and honoring the Lord as David did has proven to be a great blessing even in extremely difficult circumstances.

> "As a young Christian in college I was often on my knees asking the Lord to help with college fees and even incidentals–stockings, underwear, notebook paper and a warm scarf. The wonderful thing was that when I

sought him in prayer, he answered!

"The main building on our college campus was perched on a hill overlooking the Hudson River. The setting was beautiful. Maneuvering was more difficult. It was easy going when we walked down into the town but coming back was the struggle. Groups of students often stopped along the way to rest.

"I learned and quoted Psalm 34 on those walks up the hillside. I had no problem with verse 6: 'This poor man called, and the Lord heard him; He saved him out of all his troubles.'

"I knew then, as I know now, that anyone–man, woman, young, old, rich, poor, black or white–can call on the Lord and He will answer and meet the need.

"If you have been going through a difficult period in your life, if you have been crushed by some unkind deed, or if you have lost a loved one and are feeling the pangs of loneliness, remember the psalmist said that 'the Lord is close to the brokenhearted' (verse 18).

"Why not take refuge in him?"

Michael W. Smith has written, in *It's Time To Be Bold*, "When you're broken, God has His best chance to work. 'A wise person thinks about death, but a fool thinks only about having a good time,' Ecclesiastes 7:4. 'God whispers to us in our pleasures,' wrote C. S. Lewis in *The Problem of Pain*, 'but He shouts in our pain. Pain is God's megaphone to rouse a deaf world.' It seems that about the only time He has our complete attention is when we're in some kind of trouble.

> "I have a friend who reminds me that God wants just three things from us: bent knees, broken hearts, and wet eyes. And if He gets them, He can work wonders in our lives. It's not that God is trying to spoil our fun; it's just that He knows we're most available to Him when our pride is out of the way. The broken ground is most receptive to the seed.
>
> "Don't lose hope when you're going through the valley."

<u>Why Do We Struggle So?</u>

IF...
God is a warrior God,
God is our Great Defender,
God has promised to be with us,
fighting our battles for us,
We are partners with God in covenant,
God has promised us victory in every situation,
God has promised us light in the midst of darkness,
God has assured us we have nothing to fear,
Nothing we can do will change God's love for us,
...then why do we struggle so?
–Author unknown

Devotional thought for the day. "If we have accepted

God's forgiveness and have been released from the burdens of the past, – we will be free to do and be all that God intended. It is through a totally dedicated heart that we experience true liberation."

Harold S. Kushner, the author of the best-seller *When Bad Things Happen to Good People,* is Rabbi Laureate of Temple Israel in Natick, Massachusetts, where he served the congregation for 24 years. The following article is based on his new book–*How Good Do We Have To Be?*

> "I stood by the bed of a dying congregant and asked him if he wanted me to pray for him– or was he so angry at God for what was happening that prayer would only make him feel worse? He looked at me and said, 'No, I'm not angry at God. There have been plenty of times when I felt that I had done so many things wrong, I figured God had given up on me. But lying here in the hospital, I've felt God's presence in this room.
>
> "He went on: 'When I was young, I thought I had to be perfect for people to love me. I thought that if I ever did something wrong, their love would be withdrawn. So every time I did something wrong, I would make excuses. I would lie. I would try to find someone else to blame. I didn't realize what an unpleasant person I became when I acted that way. I thought it was my imperfection, not my defensiveness, that turned people off. But lying here in the hospital–sick and cranky and dying, but feeling God's presence in the doctors and nurses who try to help me, in the

friends and family who come to visit me–I've finally learned that you don't have to be perfect to be worth loving. I only wish I had known that sooner.'

"We need to give ourselves permission to be human, to try and then to stumble, to be momentarily weak and feel shame, but to overcome that shame with moments of strength, courage and generosity. We need to learn to define ourselves not by our worst moments but by our more typical ones. Life is not a spelling bee where one mistake wipes out all the things we have done right. Life is not a test for which the passing grade is 100 percent and anything less is a failure. Maybe when it comes to building bridges and space capsules, one mistake renders the entire project worthless. But life is so much more complicated than building bridges or space capsules that we can't expect ourselves or anyone else to do it error-free.

"Life is like the baseball season, where even the best team loses at least a third of its games and even the worst team has its days of brilliance. The goal is not to win every game, but to win more than you lose, and if you do that often enough, in the end you may find you have won it all."

When we <u>really</u> believe God means what He says, we have confidence to move ahead and do exploits. (See Joshua 10:8-14, 21, 25. Joshua had been successful fighting many battles, 11:21. Now (11:23) he's slaying giants.

Isaiah 48:17. "This is what the Lord says–your Redeemer, the Holy One of Israel. 'I am the Lord your God, Who teaches you what is best for you, Who directs you in the way you should go.'

Marjorie Holmes has written, "I am grateful, God, that I have finally come to realize Your purpose for me. Maybe because life is so filled with defeat and heartbreak, we find ourselves turning to You, yielding ourselves to Your will, fighting furiously for selfish, often empty goals. And when this happens we find that You have turned our sufferings and our failures into little stepping stones."

Jesus may be your Savior, but is He your Lord? Does He have your permission to control everything in your life? If so, you don't define the parameters of His work or the events He uses. He sets the boundaries. (James 4:13, 15)

Unbound, by Paula Kirk.

> "Lazarus had died, and Jesus hadn't been there. Both Mary and Martha, his sisters, knew that if Jesus had been there, their brother wouldn't have died. Jesus would have healed him and all would be well in their world. Now they were confused. Had their faith in Him been misplaced? Why hadn't He come earlier? What could He possibly do now?
>
> "When Jesus came, and they couldn't see beyond the grief, He stepped into their sorrow; He wept with them. He wept for them. Then He did the totally unexpected. He went to the tomb, called Lazarus out and restored him to his family and his community.

"I sometimes try to imagine what Lazarus must have looked like, staggering like a mummy from the dark of that tomb. He had been dead four days. His body was tightly wrapped in layers of cloth that bound pounds of burial spices to his body. His limbs were not free. His head was encased in a burial shroud as well. He could neither see nor speak. Yet he was alive and he knew it. He could feel life once again coursing through his body. Then he heard his much-loved Friend speak again. 'Unbind him and let him go.'

"What a perfect picture of the work Jesus does for each of His children. Because of His own resurrection, He has authority to call us to 'Come forth,' into His kingdom from the tomb of our sin and spiritual darkness. And when we do, receiving Him as Savior, He will surely say, 'Unbind him, or her, and let him loose.' We hear His voice, and no longer dead or condemned by our sin, we let Him begin to remove the baggage of the past and the evil habits that have bound us. By the power of His resurrection life, He calls us forth from the dead to set us free. He's done His part. Now we must do ours. Let's shake off the rest of our rags and embrace the power of the resurrection."

Isaiah 43:18, 19, GNB, "Do not cling to events of the past or dwell on what happened long ago. Watch for the new thing I am going to do. It is happening already–you can see it now."

Jeremiah 29:11, 12. I will bless you with a future filled with hope - a future of success, not of suffering. You will turn back to me and ask for help, and I will answer your prayers.

Joel 2:25, 26. I will repay you for the years the locusts have eaten - the great locust and the young locust, the other locusts and the locust swarm - My great army that I sent among you. You will have plenty to eat, until you are full, and you will praise the name of the Lord your God, Who has worked wonders for you; never again will My people be shamed.

Romans 8:3, 4. For what the law was powerless to do in that it was weakened by the sinful nature, God did by sending His own Son in the likeness of sinful man to be a sin offering. And so He condemned sin in sinful man, in order that the righteous requirements of the law might be fully met in us, who do not live according to the sinful nature but according to the Spirit.

MISCELLANEOUS WRITINGS FOR MEDITATION

I Asked God...

I asked God for strength, that I might achieve . . .
I was made weak, that I might learn humbly to obey.

I asked for health, that I might do greater things . . .
I was given infirmity, that I might do better things.

I asked for riches, that I might be happy . . .
I was given poverty, that I might be wise.

I asked for power, that I might have the praise of men . . .
I was given weakness that I might feel the need of God.

I asked for all things, that I might enjoy life . . .
I was given life, that I might enjoy all things.

I got nothing that I asked for, but everything I had hoped for. Almost despite myself, my unspoken prayers were answered.

I am among all men, most richly blessed!
- Anonymous

To Achieve Your Dreams, Remember Your ABCs

Avoid negative sources, people, places, things and habits.
Believe in yourself.
Consider things from every angle.
Don't give up, and don't give in.
Enjoy life today; yesterday is gone, and tomorrow may never come.
Family and friends are hidden treasures. Seek them and enjoy their riches.
Give more than you planned to give.
Hang on to your dreams.
Ignore those who try to discourage you.
Just do it!
Keep on trying. No matter how hard it seems, it will get easier.
Love yourself first and most.
Make it happen.
Never lie, cheat or steal. Always strike a fair deal.
Open your eyes and see things as they really are.
Practice makes perfect.
Quitters never win and winners never quit.
Read, study, and learn about everything important in your life.
Stop procrastinating.
Take control of your own destiny.
Understand yourself in order to better understand others.
Visualize it.
Want it more than anything.
Xccelerate your efforts.
You are unique of all God's creations. Nothing can replace you.
Zero in on your target and go for it!

Anonymous

Just For Today:

Just for today I will live through this day only. I will not brood about yesterday or obsess about tomorrow. I will not set far-reaching goals or try to overcome all my problems at once. I know that I can do something for 24 hours that would overwhelm me if I had to keep it up for a lifetime.

Just for today I will be happy. I will not dwell on thoughts that depress me. If my mind fills with clouds, I will chase them away and fill it with sunshine.

Just for today I will accept what is. I will face reality. I will correct those things I can correct, and accept those I cannot.

Just for today I will improve my mind. I will read something that requires effort, thought, and concentration. I will not be a mental loafer.

Just for today I will make a conscious effort to be agreeable. I will be kind and courteous to those who cross my path, and I will not speak ill of others. I'll improve my appearance, speak softly, and not interrupt when someone else is talking. Just for today I'll refrain from improving anybody except myself.

Just for today I will do something positive to improve my health. If I'm a smoker, I'll quit. If I'm overweight, I'll eat healthily–if only for today. And just for today, I'll get off the couch and take a brisk walk, even if it's only around the block.

Just for today I will gather the courage to do what is right and take responsibility for my own actions.
- Author Unknown

<u>After A While</u>, Veronica Shoffstall

After a while you learn the subtle difference between holding a hand and sharing a life, and you learn that love doesn't mean possession, and company doesn't mean security, and loneliness is universal.

And you learn that kisses aren't contracts, and presents aren't promises, and you begin to accept your defeats with your head up and your eyes open with the grace of a woman, not the grief of a child.

And you learn to build your hope on today as the future has a way of falling apart in mid-flight because tomorrow's ground can be too uncertain for plans, yet each step taken in a new direction creates a path toward the promise of a brighter day.

And you learn that even sunshine burns if you get too much, so you plant your own garden and nourish your own soul instead of waiting for someone to bring you flowers.

And you learn that love, true love, always has joys and sorrows, seems ever present, yet is never quite the same, becoming more than love and less than love so difficult to define.

And you learn that through it all you really can endure, that you really are strong, that you do have value, and you learn and grow with every goodbye you learn.

Press On

Nothing in the world can take the place of persistence.
Talent will not: nothing is more common than unsuccessful men with talent.
Genius will not: unrewarded genius is almost a proverb.
Education will not: the world is full of educated derelicts.
Persistence and determination alone are omnipotent.
Author unknown

Robert Schuller quotes:

"Tough times never last, but tough people do."
"Great people are ordinary people with extraordinary amounts of determination."
"When faced with a mountain **I WILL NOT QUIT.** I will keep on striving until I climb over, find a pass through, tunnel underneath, or simply stay and turn the mountain into a gold mine - with God's help.

The Victor, C. W. Longenecker

If you think you are beaten, you are.
If you think you dare not, you don't.
If you like to win but think you can't,
It's almost a cinch you won't.
If you think you'll lose, you're lost.
For out in the world we find
Success begins with a fellow's will.
It's all in the state of mind.
If you think you are outclassed, you are.
You've got to think high to rise.
You've got to be sure of yourself before
You can ever win the prize.
Life's battles don't always go

To the stronger or faster man.
But sooner or later, the man who wins
Is the man who thinks he can.

<u>The Man In The Glass</u>. Dale Wimbrow

When you get what you want in your struggle for self,
And the world makes you king for a day,
Just go to the mirror and look at yourself,
And see what *that* man has to say.
For it isn't your father or mother or wife
Whose judgement upon you must pass.
The fellow whose verdict counts most in your life
Is the one staring back from the glass.
Some people might think you're a straight-shootin' chum
And call you a wonderful guy,
But the man in the glass says you're only a bum,
If you can't look him straight in the eye.
He's the fellow to please, never mind all the rest,
For he's with you clear up to the end,
And you've passed your most dangerous, difficult test
If the guy in the glass is your friend.
You may fool the whole world down the pathway of years,
And get pats on the back as you pass,
But your final reward will be heartaches and tears
If you've cheated the man in the glass.

A well-known speaker started off his seminar by holding up a $20 bill. In the room of 200, he asked, "Who would like this $20 bill?" Hands started going up. He said, "I am going to give this $20 to one of you, but first, let me do this. He proceeded to crumple the $20 dollar bill.

He then asked, "Who still wants it?" Still the hands were up in the air. Well, he replied, "What if I do this?" And he dropped it on the ground and started to grind it into the floor with his shoe. He picked it up, now crumpled and dirty. "Now, who still wants it?" Still the hands went into the air.

My friends, we have all learned a very valuable lesson. No matter what I did to the money, you still wanted it because it did not decrease in value. It was still worth $20.

Many times in our lives, we are dropped, crumpled, and ground into the dirt by the decisions we make and the circumstances that come our way. We feel as though we are worthless. But no matter what has happened or what will happen, you will never lose your value. Dirty or clean, crumpled or finely creased, you are still priceless to those who DO LOVE you.

The worth of our lives comes not in what we do or who we know, but by WHO WE ARE. You are special. Don't EVER forget it. "

Count your blessings, not your problems. Never be afraid to try something new. And remember; amateurs built the ark, professionals built the Titanic. (Author Unknown)

From a *Dear Abby* column. "Make this new year your best one ever." (This can apply whatever the time of year!)

Let this coming year be better than all the others. Vow to do some of the things you've always wanted to do but couldn't find the time.

Call up a forgotten friend. Drop an old grudge and replace it with some pleasant memories. Share a funny story with someone whose spirits are dragging.

Vow not to make a promise you don't think you can keep. Pay a debt. Give a soft answer. Free yourself of envy and malice. Encourage some youth to do his or her best. Share your experience and offer encouragement.

Make a real effort to stay in closer touch with family and good friends. Resolve to stop magnifying small problems and shooting from the lip.

Find the time. All of us have the same allotment: 24 hours a day. Give a compliment. It could make someone's day. Think things through. Forgive an injustice. Listen more.

Apologize when you realize you were wrong. An apology never diminishes a person. It elevates him. Don't blow your own horn. If you've done something praiseworthy, someone will notice sooner or later.

Try to understand a point of view that is different from your own. Few things are 100 percent one way or another. Examine your demands on others. Lighten up. Take a quiet walk alone when you feel like blowing your top. Laugh the loudest when the joke is on you.

The sure way to have a friend is to be one. We are all connected by our humanity and our need for one another. Avoid malcontents and pessimists. They drag you down and contribute nothing. Be kind. Don't discourage a beginner from trying something risky. Nothing ventured means nothing gained. Be optimistic. The can-do spirit is the fuel that makes things go. Go to war against animosity and complacency. Express your gratitude.

Read something uplifting. Deep-six the trash. You wouldn't eat garbage; why put it in your head? Don't abandon your old-fashioned principles. They never go out of style. When courage is needed, ask yourself, 'If not me, who? If not now, when?'

Take better care of yourself. Remember, you're all you've got. Pass up that second helping. You really don't need it. Vow to eat more sensibly. You'll feel better and look better too.

Don't put up with secondhand smoke. Nobody has the right to pollute your air or give you cancer. If someone says, 'This is a free country,' remind him or her that the country may be free, but no person is free if he has a habit he can't control.

Return those books you borrowed. Reschedule that missed dental appointment. Clean out your closet. Take those photos out of the drawer and put them in an album. If you see litter on the sidewalk, pick it up instead of walking over it.

Get real. Phoniness is transparent and tiresome. Take pleasure in the beauty and the wonders of nature. A flower is God's miracle. Walk tall. Look people in the eye. Don't be bound by superstition and fear. Smile more. You'll look 10 years younger.

Don't be afraid to say, 'I love you.' Say it again. Say it still one more time. They are the sweetest words in the world.

Make this year the best ever."

Also from a *Dear Abby* column. "Five Votes of Confidence.

Today is a new day. Hence:

1. I refuse to be shackled by yesterday's failures.
2. What I don't know I will no longer allow to intimidate me. I will instead view it as an opportunity.
3. I will not allow others to define my mood, my method, my image, or my mission.
4. I will pursue a mission greater than myself by making at least one person happy that he or she saw me.
5. I will not tolerate self-pity, gossip or negativism–from myself or from others.

JUST FOR FUN! (From *USA Weekend*. 11/14-16, 2003)

"America's Pie Chart: What Yours Says About You.

No matter how flaky you are, your favorite pie broadcasts your personality. That's according to Gale Gand, executive pastry chef at Chicago's Tru restaurant, host of the Food Network's dessert-centric show Sweet Dreams, author of Gale Gand's Short and Sweet and proud user of a rolling pin passed down from her great-grandmother–a rolling pin that's turned out more than 1,200 pies in the past century.

"Gand's observations:

If your favorite pie is this, you're....

Apple	Wholesome and a bit middle-of-the-road, playing it safe.
Banana cream	An overachiever who just wants to relax and not be in charge.
Blueberry	Outdoorsy and determined.
Cherry	Oversweet, in need of tartness and passion.
Chocolate	Suave, seductive, strong, addictive.
Coconut cream	Probably a man seeking an exotic-life escape from reality.
Lemon	Bright, energetic, and sharp-tongued.
Mincemeat	An Anglophile who watches *Masterpiece Theater*, listens to NPR and fantasizes about being in England, sipping port with pie.
Peach	A sun-worshiper who's found sunshine on a pie plate.
Pecan	Simple in your tastes and seeking more sweetness in life.
Pumpkin	Attached to your past but comfy in your present.

<u>Rhubarb</u> Old-fashioned (or a total hipster).

<u>Sweet potato</u> Family-oriented, with a real sense of Southern hospitality.

Notes

CHAPTER FIFTEEN

DESIGNING MY GARDEN

Source: *Southern Living Landscape Book,* Oxmoor House.

"Each part of a well-designed landscape has its own function. The front yard reflects how you present yourself to friends, neighbors, and passersby. It should clearly guide guests to the entry. It should also anchor the house so it blends well with the natural landscape. The back yard – whether it contains a child's play area, a lush perennial border, a treasured collection of plants, beautiful garden accessories, or simply a comfortable sitting area – should be your private space. And finally, all houses need practical service areas where you can conceal items such as trash receptacles, potting benches, and tools.

"Apply your own personal touches. Don't be afraid to experiment. Dan Franklin of Atlanta said, 'One of the beauties of any garden is that it is okay for plants to have feet and be moved around until you get just the right look.' It is part of the personal design process.

"Two countries in particular affected the development of garden styles: France and England. From France came geometric gardens intersected by straight lines, formal parterres, and clipped hedges. Often concealed behind walls, these gardens depended on evergreen foliage, patterned stonework, fountains, and ornamental iron for visual impact. French garden styles are seen today in New Orleans, Mobile, Savannah and Charleston.

"England had an even greater influence, integrating the house with its natural surroundings; that a house and garden should work together. The English influence is found in the love of color and flowering plants. The English cottage garden shows a frenzy of flowers seemingly thrown together, but with carefully planned vignettes–combinations of colors and shapes conceived almost as paintings.

"On the opposite end of the spectrum is the English mixed border, a carefully orchestrated blend of annuals, perennials, bulbs, shrubs and even trees.

"In the 20th century, in the South, gardening came into its own, with manicured lawns and the use of mixed plantings, ground covers, and paved areas to reduce maintenance, adding privacy, parking, getting people to the front door comfortably and leaving room for recreation; establishing a sense of place."

In designing your garden, you may wish to heed ideas from Fran Sorin, in an article titled "A Foolproof

Flower Garden."

> "Maybe you've just moved from an apartment to your first house. Between family, work, carpooling, and everything else–has it been 12 trips to the Home Depot?–your first garden awaits your imprint. Planting flowers is a great way to exercise your creativity, but it can seem daunting to the beginner. Don't despair: The investment of time and energy will repay you in spades. After more than 20 years of designing gardens, here's my insider's guide to getting started.
>
> 1. **Know your property's relationship to the sun.** If you have a true southern exposure, you'll get direct sun most of the afternoon. A northern exposure will give you mainly shade; eastern exposure, morning sun and afternoon shade; western exposure, pretty much late-afternoon sun, with shade the rest of the day.
> 2. **Make sure the type of garden you want can be done with the amount of sun you get.** For example, although most herb and cutting gardens need direct sunlight (six hours of sun a day), woodland gardens thrive in shade. If you have a shady lot and you want a cutting garden just like the one you saw in a magazine, forget it. Instead, try to re-interpret it by using shade perennials, bulbs, and shrubs.

3. **Choose a site for your flower bed that can be viewed from inside your house.** If possible, take advantage of garden views from outdoor terraces or patios, too.
4. **Let your garden reflect your personal style, just as your indoor space does.** If you tend toward the traditional indoors, think in terms of a traditional garden with a formal, symmetrical outline, perhaps with pedestals of evergreens to add to the mood. If you lean toward a more rustic style, your outdoor space should reflect that informal feel: Let an abundance of flowers brim over the edges of the garden, and use some flea market finds as containers.
5. **When you're ready to experiment with the placement of the flower bed, lay out a hose to outline its shape and size.** (Or use spray landscape paint from a paint store.) Leave the hose in one position for a few days before deciding whether that configuration works. Geometric shapes generally indicate a formal design; irregular or island beds are more informal.
6. **When the soil has warmed up and is not too soggy, you can dig the bed.** First, remove the grass–roots and all–with a spade, or use an herbicide (like Round-Up) or an organic grass killer. Then rototill the area or turn it over with a fork. At least

12 inches of good organic matter should be laid on top of the existing soil. Once you've raked the organic matter evenly across the bed, edge the perimeter with a sharp spade to give it a professional, crisp finish.

7. **The most effective gardens are simple ones that follow the adage "Less is more."** Select plants of various shapes and textures that bloom at different times of the gardening season and that resist disease and drought. Limit your palette to two or three colors. I like to work with combinations of three plants to create a vignette.
8. **Plant a lot of each specimen.** The repetition of specimens and colors soothes the eye and paves the way for a more glorious design. I plant a minium of seven of each specimen in a small garden bed, and up to 20-something of each in an expansive area.
9. **Plant in a flowing or wavelike pattern.** Play around with the plants while they are still in their pots, positioning them around your garden bed to see how they look before you actually plant them. Some of my greatest moments of inspiration occur when I make last-minute changes.
10. **Spread mulch as soon as possible after planting (no more than 2 inches thick).** Do it carefully,

to avoid damaging the plants.

11. **Until the plants are settled in about two weeks), I water every third day** early in the morning, 30 to 45 minutes at a time, with a soaker hose or a rotating sprinkler.
12. **Over the remainder of the spring (in cool regions, into the early summer), fill in bare areas with exuberant summer bulbs or tubers** such as dahlias, cannas, elephant ears, oxalis and colocasias, and annual plants or seeds that can be scratched right into your garden soil.
13. **To give the plants extra 'oomph,' spray them with an organic fertilizer,** such as fish fertilizer, once every four weeks, [preferably first thing in the morning when it's cool–never when the temperature is above 80 degrees.
14. **Be patient.** Plants won't fully mature for a good two to three years. Enjoy the process and keep notes on the plant combinations that give you great pleasure. I think you will be surprised how often you use them as you continue to create new gardens."

Taken from *Southern Living* magazine, June, 2003, Special Section.

"A well-loved garden can bring you riches both inside and out.

"Some of us garden so that our yards will be filled with lush grass and vibrant colors. Others try to produce giant red tomatoes and fresh, healthy food for our families. Then there are those who garden to fill their lives with peace and quiet. Regardless of the outcome, this activity provides a glorious way to enjoy life and make the world a better place. Gardening can:

"**Stimulate the mind.** Most people think of gardening as a physical activity, centered around digging holes and watering plants. But there's a more subtle side that often has a bigger impact on the ultimate success of a garden than the many hours of labor spent outside. Understanding the environment you live in and the growth requirements of the plants you wish to use is essential information every gardener should have. Spending time researching these facts can eventually save a lot of money and sweat. It will also provide your mind with the stimulus it needs to operate effectively.

"Gardening can be a great door for discovering the wonders of the natural world. Simply following a plant's cycle–from germination to setting seed–can uncover some of the most fantastic biological secrets. Letting your curiosity lead you down a garden path can reveal the amazing partnership between insects, plants, and the soil in which they grow. Take a moment to appreciate the shape of an iris. In doing so, gardening can become more than a physical endeavor.

"Reduce stress. A well-designed garden should be a refuge from the things that drive you crazy–not a source of more insanity. Think about the yard tasks you love to perform, then create a garden that affords ample opportunities for you to do them. If mowing the lawn is the bane of your weekend, reduce the size of your lawn so a couple of minutes with a push mower is all it takes to keep it cut. Or plant a slower-growing kind of grass and fertilize it less frequently. If even the smallest lawn drives you over the edge, plant a ground cover such as mondo grass or vinca, which will look great and require pruning only once a year.

"Gardens offer great stress relief by letting you focus on small tasks, allowing larger concerns to fade away. Time can take on an entirely different meaning while dividing and replanting bulbs. The speed of life slows to match the pace of the botanical world, and what seemed like pressing concerns outside the garden quickly reprioritize.

"Creating community. One great way to get to know your neighbors is to spend a few hours out in the front yard. Inevitably, folks will stop to chat about successes and challenges. It may be the start of something beautiful.

"Another way gardening brings people together is through the community garden movement. If you lack space in your own yard or simply want to enjoy the company of others while working with plants, find a community garden in your neighborhood–or start one yourself.

"Slow down to reflect. As with life, gardening is best when viewed as a journey, not a destination. If you can learn to enjoy each step of the process, your garden will become a source of peace, and beauty will naturally follow." - Edwin Marty

SPIRITUAL APPLICATION

God is my Master Designer and Gardener.

Ephesians 2:10 NIV "For we are God's workmanship, created in Christ Jesus to do good works, which God prepared in advance for us to do."

Jeremiah 29:11 NIV "For I know the plans I have for you, declares the Lord, plans to prosper you and not to harm you, plans to give you hope and a future."

Psalm 139:16b NIV "All the days ordained for me were written in Your book before one of them came to be."

All that we have studied and discussed in the previous fourteen chapters are a part of designing your spiritual garden: soil, what's growing, fertilizers and nourishment, companion planting, irrigating, mulching and watering, pruning, the "inhabitants," tools, seasons and weather, harvesting and reaping, the kind of clothing we wear when "gardening," and ridding of wildernesses.

I have read that no garden is ever finished, and I know that applies spiritually too. We will not be "finished" until the Lord is ready to take us to His heavenly home.

Think about what you would like to see in the garden of your heart. Following are a few articles I have collected, many from our own newspaper. They may contain some ideas for planting in your garden.

Worst bad hair day can become beautiful time for ministry. The Reverend Martha Sterne, rector of St. Andrew's Episcopal Church in Maryville, Tennessee:

"I have always had difficult hair. I want to be grateful for the hair God has given me, so I'll just use the word difficult, meaning frizzy or flat, depending on the weather and my current life stance – more like a mood ring than a reliable head of hair."

In the article, this rector goes on to tell about her

difficult hair, the many beauticians she's patronized and the way she has observed them "ministering" to their clients.

She concluded the lengthy article by telling about Mary, a hairdresser who, upon having a client describe a situation in her life which had left her distraught, knelt in front of the client to listen, giving her her undivided attention.

She said, "And I left – love and comfort and common sense flowing through the room like the balm of Gilead."

"You know the church could do worse than be an 'inner beauty' shop – a place where we can look into the mirror together and see each other's potential and belovedness. The church could do worse than be a place where love is shared and truth is told and the beauty of becoming is the work of the community."

In the *Faith Today* column, *The Daily Times*, Maryville, Tennessee, David Anderson wrote, Practice patience with God.

> "Give me patience, Lord, and GIVE IT TO ME NOW! So goes the saying. Think of all the things that might have been better if we had only expended a little more patience with an estranged spouse or child. How many friendships have been wasted because one or both persons acted with pride and anger rather than according to patience and love? Too many, I fear.
>
> "The Lord revealed Himself to Moses as 'compassionate, and gracious, slow to anger, and abounding in loving kindness and truth.' (Exodus 34, NAS). I cannot begin to tell how thankful I am that the Lord has been patient with me. Sometimes I feel like a work in process that will just never come to

completion, pinched off from a piece of clay and filled with defects for Him to remove and rework. Yet I am very thankful that He persistently reworks rather than casting aside. The patience of God moves me very deeply at times.

"Then I must consider, 'Well, just how patient have I been with God? How have I returned His patience toward me?' Not as well, I'm afraid. Doubtless we need patience with each other, and doubtless we need the patience of God with us. Yet it is surprising how much the Scripture refers to us 'waiting upon the Lord.' It may well be that refusing to wait upon the Lord lay at the root of many sins of the ancient people of God. Sadly, that same fact seems frightfully true today.

"Psalm 37 has a great deal to say about patience with our God and waiting upon the Lord. 'Fret not yourself because of evildoers;' it teaches us, 'Trust in the Lord, and do good.' But when we are wronged, everything within us cries out for revenge! Do we have the patient strength to trust the Lord and simply continue to do good? 'Commit your way to the Lord' the psalm continues, 'trust in Him, and He will act.' That can be tough to do. It requires patience, not only with those who wrong us, but with the Lord, while we wait for Him to act on our behalf. Again, the psalm admonishes the people of God to, 'Be still before the Lord and wait patiently for Him. Wait for the Lord and keep His way.' The salvation of God's people comes from God alone not only spiritually, but sometimes quite literally. When we forget that, we set ourselves up for many hurtful experiences. When we patiently keep the ways of Jesus we testify silently, but eloquently, of our belief in the righteousness and the loving care of the Lord. God notices. God cares.

"Nothing in God's Word teaches us that we will never suffer. Quite the contrary, we are pretty much assured that we will suffer. The question for us to consider then, is how we will respond in the context of that suffering."

Another article in *The Daily Times* from August 2003, is written by Melanie McGhee, <u>Say thank you every single day.</u>

"Expressing genuine gratitude to people we encounter as we move through our days and nights has a tremendous impact on the quality of our relationships. This bears out in both personal and professional relationships. And it's easy. Saying thank you does not take a lot of time or energy. It is simply a matter of noticing.

"Consider taking the time to notice those around you. Notice how the people in your life daily perform small actions to make your life a little easier.

"Thankfulness weaves a bond of trust between you and others. Simply acknowledging the goodness in life seems to tune our attention to the good. It is easier then to find reasons to trust. Acknowledgment, the expression of gratitude, strengthens our ability to recognize what is right in life.

"Moreover, deciding to look for ways to feel and express gratitude can bring you into the magic of the present moment. I find that I move more slowly and feel greater peace when I am on the lookout for ways to acknowledge others. This has even spread to looking out for ways to acknowledge and thank myself.

"I find it intriguing how telling myself 'thank you' creates a sublime sense of peacefulness within. Just as thanking others for their small kindnesses and everyday contributions to my life increases the sense of well-being in the relationship, thanking myself for the small things I do every day increases my own sense of well-being.

"Every day, there is someone to thank. Find them and thank them. Look at all that you do for yourself to make your life work. Thank yourself. Just for a while, play with thankfulness. Take gratitude to new heights and see where it takes you."

C. S. Lewis, in a letter dated August 10, 1958, wrote "We ought to give thanks for all fortune: if it is 'good,' because it is good, if 'bad,' because it works in us patience, humility and the contempt of this world and the hope of our eternal country."

In *Parade* magazine March, 1997, Ralph Fiennes was being interviewed and quoted. He was asked, "Don't fame and success isolate you from what you were before and those you loved?"

Mr. Fiennes replied, "Success? Well I don't know quite what you mean by success. Material success? Worldly success? Personal, emotional success? The people I consider successful are so because of how they handle their responsibilities to other people, how they approach the future, people who have a full sense of the value of their life and what they want to do with it. I call people 'successful' not because they have money or their business is doing well but because, as human beings, they have a fully developed sense of being alive and engaged in a lifetime task of collaboration with other human beings–their mothers and fathers, their family, their friends, their loved ones, the friends who are dying, the friends who are being born.

"Success? Don't you know it is all about being able to extend love to people? Really. Not in a big, capital-letter sense but in the everyday; little by little, task by task, gesture by gesture, word by word."

A Prayer For Parents

"Oh God, make me a better parent. It is the most important job in the world and one for which there is no prior training.

"Help me to understand my children, to listen patiently to what they have to say and to respond to their questions kindly.

"Keep me from interrupting and contradicting them.

"Help me to be as courteous to them as I would have them be to me.

"Give me the courage to confess my sins against my children and the generosity of spirit to ask them for forgiveness when I know I have done wrong.

"Forbid that I should laugh at their mistakes or resort to shame and ridicule.

"Oh Lord, reduce the meanness in me.

"May I cease to nag. When I am out of sorts, help me, please, to hold my tongue and keep my temper under control.

"Blind me to the insignificant shortcomings of my children, and help me to see the good things they do.

"Give me a ready word for honest praise. Make me ever mindful that they need the nurturing that comes with encouragement and appreciation for their small successes.

"Help me remember that my children are only children so that I may not expect from them the judgment of adults.

"Allow me not to rob them of the opportunity to wait on themselves, to think for themselves, and to make their own mistakes. "Forbid that I should ever punish them as a means of ridding myself of anger and frustration. Help me to exercise reason and control.

"May I grant them all wishes that are sensible and have the courage to withhold a privilege when I know it might do them harm.

"Make me fair and just, considerate and companionable, so they will have genuine esteem, respect and affection for me.

"Make me fit to be loved and imitated by my children, for this is the greatest compliment of all."

A song, <u>Pursuing Your Presence</u>

To think that there were moments
You were near without my knowing,
makes me realize the times I missed with You.
Forgive me for my busy-ness
and all those wasted hours
spent pursuing things I thought I had to do.
I don't want to miss Your footsteps
when You're walking in my garden.
I don't want to lose a moments time with You.
Make my heart so tender
it will hear Your softest whisper.
Your presence is the life that I pursue.

Chorus: Pursuing Your presence,
I run to Your presence,

undone by Your presence.
What can I do but bow before You
and worship Your presence,
and run to Your presence,
undone by Your presence.
What can I do but bow before You
and worship Your presence

I conclude with this poem, Garden Musings, by Peggy Stevens.

I have a garden on the land,
Well-cultivated and well-planned.
Neat rows of vegetables and greens,
With vines of grapes to form a screen.

The fence row boasts hybrid sweet peas,
While hollyhocks nod with the breeze.
Dwarf marigolds and lines of phlox
Mingle with blue forget-me-nots.

I have a garden in my heart–
With verdant soil my thoughts impart;
I watch for prejudice and greed
That choke as surely as a weed.

A furrow of kind deeds is there,
And flourishing in sun and air,
A row of hope, a courage crop,
And vines of wisdom creep on top.

All this is nurtured with great care
By thoughtfulness and faith and prayer.
Each day on bended knee I toil,
In gardens of the heart and soil.

May your heart be a well-tended garden where the Lord will find fragrance and beauty. May there be fruit to nourish all those who travel through your life.

God bless you!

Notes

WHO AM I IN CHRIST?

I AM
A child of God,
Saved by grace through faith,
Redeemed from the hand of the foe,
An heir of eternal life, forgiven,
Led by the Spirit of God, a new creature,
Redeemed from the curse of the law,
Kept in safety wherever I go,
Strong in the Lord and in His mighty power,
Living by faith and not by sight,
Rescued from the dominion of darkness,
Justified, an heir of God and co-heir with Christ,
Blessed with every spiritual blessing,
An overcomer by the blood of the Lamb
and the word of my testimony,
The light of the world, an imitator of God,
Healed by His wounds,
Being transformed by the renewing of my mind,
Heir to the blessings of Abraham,
Doing all things through Christ who gives me strength,
More than a conqueror

THE CHRISTIAN'S DECLARATION OF INDEPENDENCE

I am free from failure for "I can do all things through Christ which strengthens me." Philippians 4:13
I am free from want for "my God shall supply all my need according to His riches in glory by Christ Jesus." Philippians 4:19
I am free from fear for "God has not given us the spirit of fear, but of power, and of love, and of a sound mind." II Timothy 1:7
I am free from doubt for "God has given to every man the measure of faith." Romans 12:3
I am free from weakness, "for the Lord is the strength of my life." Psalm 27:1 and "the people that know their God shall be strong and do exploits." Daniel 11:32
I am free from the power of satan, "for greater is He that is in me than he that is in the world." 1 John 4:4
I am free from defeat, "for God always causes me to triumph in Christ Jesus." II Corinthians 2:14
I am free from ignorance, "for Christ Jesus is made unto me wisdom from God." 1 Corinthians 1:30
I am free from sin, "for the blood of Jesus Christ cleanses me from all sin." 1 John 1:7
I am free from worry, "for I am to cast my cares upon Him." 1 Peter 5:7
I am free from bondage, "for where the Spirit of the Lord is, there is liberty." II Corinthians 3:17
I am free from condemnation, "for there is therefore now no condemnation to them which are in Christ Jesus." Romans 8:1

____

Signature

About The Author

Bonnie J. Lee is a resident of Maryville, in East Tennessee, a pastor's wife, and Master Gardener. She and her husband, Ted, live on over eleven acres that they have cleared, cleaned, and planted. Bonnie would rather be outside digging in the dirt, pulling weeds, transplanting, landscaping, and creating her own garden of Eden than most other activities. As of this writing, she and Ted are preparing to build another home on their property, and so she is busy planning and planting new gardens even before the house is completed.

Since putting together this Bible study, she has had the wonderful privilege of teaching it in many churches of various denominations. Her love of gardening and gift of teaching the Word of God have enlarged her territory. She doesn't let her age dictate any thought of retiring and remains excited about imparting truth that has challenged and changed her own life.

DISCLAIMER

For a number of years, the author has collected material used in this book. Her intention was to only use it for the classes she has taught.

When the idea was born to put the material in a book, there was no way to completely "track down" the originating publishers. However, credit has been given to the authors if their names were included in the sources (i.e., newspapers, magazines). Because the information may have been clipped from its source, sometimes the dates were no longer available.

www.ingramcontent.com/pod-product-compliance
Lightning Source LLC
Chambersburg PA
CBHW022116080426
42734CB00006B/154

9781928672043